WRITING AS A BUSINESS

PRODUCTION, DISTRIBUTION, AND MARKETING

TROY LAMBERT

UNBOUND
PUBLISHING

Copyright ©2019 Troy Lambert and Unbound Publishing, All Rights Reserved

This book cannot be copied or distributed without permission of the author and publisher. You may quote from this book for the purpose of reviews and sharing with others. If you have any questions or need multiple copies for educational or other purposes, please contact Unbound Media at info@unboundmedia.com.

Although the author and publisher have made every effort to ensure the information in this book was correct at the time of publication, the author and publisher do not assume and hereby disclaim any liability to any party for any loss, damage, or disruption caused by errors or omissions. Your success as an author depends on your hard work, and independent research regarding your genre and niche.

INTRODUCTION

"When a writer is born into a family, the family is finished."

— Czeslaw Milosz

"Who wants to become a writer? And why? Because it's the answer to everything.... It's the streaming reason for living. To note, to pin down, to build up, to create, to be astonished at nothing, to cherish the oddities, to let nothing go down the drain, to make something, to make a great flower out of life, even if it's a cactus."

—Enid Bagnold

When I sit down with anyone who approaches me and says "I want to write for a living" I offer them exactly this advice: Do something else. Do something your family can get behind, like being a lawyer, leaving your profession as a chemistry teacher to cook meth and "Break Bad", or even become a clown who only performs at kids' birthday parties. You know, something respectable.

The reason is this writing thing is difficult. You have to treat your passion, something you enjoy, as a business, which means much of your time you will spend on other things besides writing. Because if you write a book, or want to write for magazines, or whatever writing career path you choose, you will spend only around half your time, maybe less, writing, and the rest on nurturing your career, or the business of writing.

That is because of one simple thing: when you publish anything and want to sell it, you have started a small business. You are an entrepreneur. This is the same whether you are published by a traditional publisher or self-published, or both. We will cover those things in detail later in this book, but for now it is enough to say if you don't embrace the business side of writing, you probably won't ever make enough money to break even, let alone be a success and write for a living.

There are those of you who will say you don't care about making a living as a writer, and I will doubt your word right away if you are reading this book, but also I will ask you two more questions: Do you want other people to read your work? Why you are writing?

Most of us who write feel we have something vital to share with the world. Whether that is a story or stories, a message of hope or our own story of victory, the reason we take it from our minds and commit it to paper (pixels more often than not), is because we want others to read, understand, and apply that message. Most times with fiction, we may just want people to read and enjoy our stories.

Either way, the method people use to discover your stories is to purchase them or even download them for free if you really don't care about making money. To do that, they must discover them. This means you must distribute and market them. This does not happen organically, because no writer anywhere knows enough people to sell enough of their books to be a bestseller or even close. They need other people to sell their books for them.

The problem with many writers of all types is they get stuck in the production phase of writing as a business. Often, they never even fully complete that process, let alone move on to distribution and marketing.

In this book we will focus on writing for authors, those who have created a book or books they want to sell. The same principles apply to companies who have eBooks they want to sell or get people to download. The same basic principles with some tweaks apply to those who write articles, poetry, short stories, and more. We will explore these in less detail, but in conjunction with the rest of our discussion.

The essential point of this work is to help you, a writer, whether you are an aspiring writer or a seasoned professional, understand writing is a business. There are three parts to that business, each with many facets. They are production, distribution, and marketing. They can be basically defined in this way.

- **Production:** This is the process of **taking your idea and formatting it into a marketable product** whether that is a book, article, poem, or short story.
- **Distribution:** This is the process of getting your product into the hands of readers.
- **Marketing:** This process is how you let people know where you have distributed your work.

In the next several pages, we will talk about each of these aspects of the business of writing in detail. For your first reading, I'd suggest you read through the whole book, front to back. Then go back and skip around as you need to re-reading the parts that are most applicable to your situation and writing career.

As serious as I am when I tell new writers to do something else, what I really mean is writing as a business is hard. It takes work. If you can do something else, do it. You will save yourself hours of heartache and sorrow, because you are taking something you love, your passion, and making it into a job. This is challenging not only mentally, but physically and spiritually.

However, if you, like me, find you really aren't that good at anything else, and you **need** to do this for a living, and find a way to make it work, read on. You will gain a satisfaction known only to a select few in the world, have hours of joy to offset the frustration, and those around you will find you a livable and tolerable person.

Ready? Want to follow the path of making a living as a writer and treating writing as the business it is? Then turn the page. We will start with the mostly fun part: production.

PART ONE

PRODUCTION

"Write. Rewrite. When not writing or rewriting, read. I know of no shortcuts."

—Larry L. King

"I do not over-intellectualize the production process. I try to keep it simple: Tell the damned story."

—Tom Clancy

"One thing that helps is to give myself permission to write badly. I tell myself that I'm going to do my five or 10 pages no matter what, and that I can always tear them up the following morning if I want. I'll have lost nothing—writing and tearing up five pages would leave me no further behind than if I took the day off."

—Lawrence Block

Like any other business, the business of writing has three parts: production, distribution, and marketing. The first one we will tackle is production. This portion is also broken into several parts.

- **Writing:** To produce something, you will have to write some words. We'll tackle that aspect of production first.
- **Rewriting or Revision:** This is what you do to your writing when it is done but before you send it on to an editor.
- **Hiring an Editor:** Nope, you can't just edit your own stuff. You need to hire someone to do it for you unless you are being traditionally published. Even if you are pitching to agents and editors, you want to pitch your best work, so hiring an editor is just best-practice.
- **Sourcing a Book Cover:** If you're self-publishing, you must do this. Like editing, you probably cannot create your own covers and do it well. There are very few exceptions to this rule.
- **Formatting:** This is the process of making the inside of the book easy to read with the right fonts on any device or in print form. You can learn to do this yourself for the various formats, or you can hire someone. We will look at the pros and cons of both.
- **Uploading your work:** Uploading to various sites and arranging for Print on Demand (POD) or for large print runs.

As mentioned before, this is taking your idea and transforming it into a product you can sell. Over the next few chapters, we will engage each of these concepts individually.

CHAPTER ONE

PRODUCTION STARTS WITH WRITING SOME WORDS

"A WRITER REPORTS on the universe. When he presents his credentials, the gates of heaven and hell are equally opened to him. He can hear the devil's defense and god's accusations. The guards at the king's heart let him in. The writer can be anything and anyone he wants. When he writes he is a god, he creates."

— *Bangambiki Habyarimana*, Pearls of Eternity

This is the stage at which you plagiarize the alphabet: you actively rearrange those 26 letters into some thoughts all your own. It does not matter at this point what kind of book you are writing. In order to proceed with any of the next steps, you need some words strung together in a manner your target audience can understand and will want to read.

How do you do this writing thing? Maybe at this stage, you just have a vague idea. Perhaps you have an outline or even an assignment. No matter what you are writing, there are some keys to finishing the story.

Write Quickly

Your first draft should be written quickly. The first draft of a novel length work should take you no more than six to nine months. Why that number?

Every writer writes from the heart, and over time your heart changes. So does the rest of you. Think about how much you have changed just over the last year. Now think about how much you have changed over the last five years. If you take three to five years to write a novel, you are a different person by the time you finish. Your voice has changed because your heart has changed. This means the editing process will be that much more difficult, unless you edit as you go - something you should not do - see the next point in this chapter.

The point you need to take away is you should complete any writing work as quickly as possible, while your mind is fresh in the subject and your thoughts are focused. The more times you go away from them then go back, the more likely it is your thoughts will become jumbled.

Do Not Edit as You Go

Yes, you can backspace, or quickly correct the spelling the squiggly red line shows you, but do not go back and rewrite until you have written "the end." The temptation is real, and some will tell you editing as you go is perfectly okay, but as someone who has edited over 50 full-length manuscripts and several smaller ones over the last several years, I can tell you that I can tell when a writer went back and rewrote a section. How?

Because doing so interrupts your flow. When you start to write again after editing, your voice will change slightly. Usually, this causes you to make errors—small ones, but you take a few moments, or paragraphs, to get back into your story or thoughts. You will end up cutting some of these words later. It's inevitable.

For example, if you wrote this:

"Can we cut the chatter? I want to hear if something is coming," Jim said. *Or if we need to go backwards really fast,* he said to himself.

"You bet. Last thing I want to be known as is a big blabbermouth. I could go on and on about mining. Talk for hours about what we do. If you think I'm running off at the mouth, you just tell me, and I'll keep my talk to myself. I worked with a guy down here once who didn't shut up for damn near the whole—"

"Dex?"

"Yeah?"

"Shut up, okay?"

You might be tempted to go back and re-write part of the dialogue. But the way it came out of your head flowed well, and when you make everything grammatically correct and eliminate contractions, suddenly the dialogue doesn't sound natural anymore. Don't do it.

Editing as you go increases the length of the editing process, since your editor has to edit out poor transitions or unnatural dialogue, smooth them over, then attempt to recreate the flow that was already there before you paused your writing process to go back and make corrections. The more an editor has to work on your manuscript, the more they charge, if you are hiring a freelance editor before entering your path to publication.

Hemmingway said you should "write drunk, edit sober." It takes time to go from one to the other. It has also been said you should "write with the door closed, edit with the door open." Never edit with the door partway open. What are we doing, heating (or cooling) the whole world with our words? All joking aside, be either writing or editing, never both at the same time on the same project.

Fiction Outlining and Research

There is often a debate between outliners and pantsters, those who research and outline ahead of time versus those who write until the end with little or no outline and save the research and outlining for the rewrite.

For instance, you might want your murderer or even your protagonist to have a certain type of gun they carry. If you are an outliner, you probably have researched this ahead of time, and already know what you will use in your story. If you are a pantster, you might just write TYPE OF GUN HERE in all caps so you will see it when you do revisions and come back to add the more detailed description later.

Outliners: These writers have every twist and turn of the story planned out before they even begin to write, some of them down to the outline of chapters and scenes. However, most will tell you this outline, however detailed or loose, is done before they ever sit down to write.

Once they start writing, they do not go back to re-outline or do more research. They simply write until the end and then go back and make corrections. Many outliners will even confess that things do not always turn out how they outlined them. Characters tend to have a mind of their own and take the story their own direction, especially in more character driven stories.

Pantsters: These writers sit down with an idea and a general direction, writing by the seat of their pants (thus the name pantsters). They start to write and follow the story and the characters wherever they go. With no outline in mind, they truly experience their book or story along with the characters.

This is also sometimes called discovery writing, because you discover the story as you go, like wandering through a strange house with a flashlight, but no real idea of where you are going.

Does this make a mess sometimes? Yes. If the writer gets distracted at some point, they can follow an aspect of the story that goes nowhere and have to backtrack and delete it later, in the editing process.

This type of writing can produce spectacular stories. Think of *Lord of the Rings* (outlined) vs. *Christine* by Stephen King (pantster). Each writer must gauge for themselves how much they can free-flow their plot, and how much structure they need to make their stories work.

"Outlines are the last resource of bad fiction writers who wish to God they were writing masters' theses."

~ *Stephen King*

Either way, as a punster or as an outliner, it is vital that both types of writers write from beginning until the very end.

The Mixer: Some writers start as pantsters, but part way through the book, they outline the rest of the story to make sure they get where they are going.

This is perhaps the most common type of writer I have come across. They blend the two techniques of writing.

How long do they free-write before they outline? It varies. Some start with a loose outline and tighten the structure as they go. Others create the outline when they are done with the story during the re-writing process, to make sure they have included all the elements they need, and that the story follows a good structure.

No matter what your method, writers write from the beginning until the very end. The best first drafts are done quickly, and they are re-written then edited only after that initial draft is done.

It pays to remember at this point that all rough drafts are crap. You cannot look at your first draft and get discouraged. That is like looking at flour, eggs, oil, some cocoa, and milk on the kitchen counter, tasting some of each, then saying, "Wow, my chocolate cake tastes horrible."

You wouldn't taste a cake before it is done. So, likewise, don't judge your writing during the drafting stages.

Non-fiction Outlining and Research

Non-fiction is an entirely different type of writing, and research and outlining are a must.

Generally, most non-fiction is linear in some way: usually time or the ordered steps in a process. Often if the order is not followed, the results are disastrous. Think of a recipe book or automotive repair manual: do the steps in the wrong order or add a "flashback" to what you should have done in step three when you are now on step six will not work.

Again, this depends on the writer and what you are writing about. Almost without exception though, you cannot be a pure pantster and write good non-fiction.

As an example, let's talk about writing memoirs: If anyone tells you, they are writing their memoir and have no outline, it usually becomes something called "creative nonfiction". You can almost guarantee there are errors in the story, and part of the story has been fictionalized at some point.

With few exceptions, memoir must be written with a linear structure of some sort. Yes, there can be flashbacks (only if they are done well), but there must be a structure to those too.

Now, you could start writing stories that will fit in your memoir without an outline, and you might even get things written, but your final book will take longer to assemble than if you would have started with a solid direction and goals in mind. It is the same with other topics. While you can write some things out of order, if you already know where they should be placed when they are complete, it will speed the assembly of your book and the final editing process.

For the most part, write your draft of nonfiction quickly for the same reason you write your fiction quickly. But there is more leeway with non-fiction. You might need to do extensive research as you go, of take a break from your memoir when things get to emotional or personal.

As with any rule, there are always exceptions and there will be those who tell you about how they have done things differently, but especially when you are first starting out, it's better to keep things simple, and discover what rules you can break as you grow as an author.

Next, we will talk about the keys to writing quickly. Here they are, briefly. We will cover each in detail in the next post.

- **Write every day:** Even if you only get a page or two completed, write something.
- **Have a writing schedule:** Even if it is as simple as 15 minutes a day, have a time that is your writing time, and stick with it.
- **Allow yourself the freedom to write more:** If you are into the flow of the story, keep writing. Don't stop

because a certain amount of time has passed. Follow the flow if you can.

- **Leave yourself hanging:** Stop on a cliffhanger if you can rather than finishing a chapter. It will be easier for you to get back into the flow the next day, and you will want to.

Next, we'll talk about how to follow these keys, and what they really mean to you and your daily routine.

CHAPTER TWO

HOW TO WRITE MORE, FASTER

"WRITING IS a sickness only cured by writing."

— *Niall Williams*, History of the Rain

"10 Steps to Becoming a Better Writer

Write.

Write more.

Write even more.

Write even more than that.

Write when you don't want to.

Write when you do.

Write when you have something to say.

Write when you don't.

Write every day.

Keep writing."

— *Brian Clark*

We ended the last chapter on a cliffhanger, something you should always do to yourself. I mean, it is great advice to write some words. If you are going to have a writing-based product to sell, you need to have something written.

However, the first step in production is where writers often get tripped up. They get caught up in the idea of selling books, especially when they first become excited about writing for a living: They get so busy creating an author platform, getting their website ready, and being sucked into social media (Oy!) that they neglect the writing part of the business. That is like putting the cart before the horse.

Before you know it, they wake up realizing their novel is stale. All the while, they have not posted an article on their blog or sent an outreach to a new blogging site in weeks. Here is the simple truth of the matter: You are a writer when you write. If you're not writing, it is harder for you to think of yourself as a writer, which can eat away at your confidence.

For example, if you are a server, but suddenly for a couple of weeks, you don't go in to the restaurant or bar where you work and actually wait on customers, are you still a server? Possibly, depending on how understanding your employer is, but spend enough time away from it, and you will have a hard time getting back into the swing of things.

How do you make sure this tragedy does not happen to you? Here are some obvious tips, but ones writers often neglect.

Write Every Day

I have many aspiring writers tell me they do not have to write every day, and they are absolutely right. You can go for days without writing. Once you embrace writing as a profession, you can't help but write every day.

Why? Writing, or engaging in any creatively based activity, changes something in your brain. It releases chemicals that make you happy when you write, and when you don't, depression, anxiety, or anger can take the place of that happiness. In my professional experience, there is no one worse to be around than a writer who is not actually writing.

Also, when you write every day, your brain changes the way it processes creativity: It thinks differently as you grow the habit of your craft, establishing new pathways for those creative neurons to travel down. Nearly every professional writer I know writes something nearly every day. Even on vacation or their "day off" they are keeping to their craft, strengthening their habit. It is not because we have to: It is because the more you write, the more you want to. This is the key to writing as a living, it has to be something you love. If it isn't, you should do something else.

Try it. I have never found any true writer who after giving daily writing an honest try, did not find the practice had not dramatically changed the process for them. Of course, there is a caveat here: I am talking to writers who want to write for a living. You can't go long without going to work before you get fired or start to go hungry because there is no money coming in. If writing is going to be your job, you have to go to work every day.

Have A Writing Schedule

I have heard all of your excuses. My kids, their school, housework, the laundry, you have five cats, four dogs, and your poor neighbor needed help with cleaning their gutters: How could I possibly write every day? I am going to be frank and potentially offensive.

All of your excuses are crap. Nearly every writer I know who does write every day, who does it for a living, did not start out that way. They had full-time jobs, wives, kids, and pets just like you do. They started to write every day anyway.

How? They set a time, usually early in the morning or late at night, and wrote at least for a little while no matter what else was happening in their lives. Read that last sentence again. They set aside a time and wrote something, even a single page, no matter what else was happening in their lives.

It can be a page in a short story. A page in a future article. A page in a novel. Three-hundred and sixty-five days of writing one page a day means you'll have a full-length novel completed in a single year. Stop telling me how busy you are, and that you do not have time to write. Set a schedule and keep it.

If your first schedule does not work for you, find one that does. Find your optimal time when everyone else is either gone or asleep and stick to your schedule no matter what. Set goals. Have hard word counts, timelines, or pages you need to meet before you let yourself get up from your writing appointment. Do it.

There are some exceptions to this rule. As you become a more seasoned writer you will be able to take time off, take breaks between books, and even keep a different writing schedule that works for you. However, for new writers who are just starting out, write every single day. Once you get to know your muse, and it gets to know you, you'll be able to figure out how to take days off without disrupting your workflow.

Allow Yourself the Freedom to Write More

Wait a minute. I just spent a whole bunch of words trying to convince you to write every day, and schedule that time, keeping it sacred. Now I am telling you to give yourself the freedom to write more?

That's right. If your goal is a page a day, or ten pages, if you get into writing and things are really flowing, keep it going if at all possible. Why? Because those are the best writing days. That feeling of being in the zone is what many of us writers live for.

On those days when the words flow from your fingers quickly and easily and your fingers fly over the keyboard, keep going. Write as much as you can as fast as your ability allows. That will probably be some of your best writing and stopping can kill your spirit. If your flow is interrupted in those moments, you may even get frustrated with the interrupter or even anxious.

Good. That means you are on the right track and your writing habit is solidifying. Control your aggravation, give yourself permission to roll with it. Also, it is important that you give yourself the freedom to write more when life is going well by taking advantage of opportunities that allow you to immerse yourself in your muse.

No matter how long you have been at this, there are days when the words do not flow as easily as they do other times. Do not mistake this for writer's block. Once you finish reading this book, you will never be allowed to claim it or blame it, again. Sometimes writing is hard, so when it is easy, go with it.

Especially when you first start out, or when there are many distractions in your life, you will struggle to keep to your daily writing schedule. Write anyway.

Leave Yourself Hanging

Earlier in this chapter, we talked about ending your writing on a cliffhanger. Even if you get on one of the beautiful rolls mentioned above, where your words are flowing like the water over Niagara Falls, when you stop, leave yourself hanging. Stop writing at the point where you are excited about writing what comes next. Whether you are excited about the next point you are making in your non-fiction book, the next event in your memoir, or the nail-biting end of a chapter in fiction. I have heard of writers who stop in the middle of a sentence at the end of each writing session.

If you are excited about what is coming next, you will anxious to sit down and write again, anticipating the next session instead of dreading it. Make no mistake, writing is work. It is a job; however, you can make it much more enjoyable for yourself.

Set Deadlines

No matter how much you want your writing to be free flowing, you still need to have deadlines. Deadlines keep a writer focused on the end game, a place to ensure you have an eye on tying up loose ends. Be the deadline is coming from a publisher or it is self-imposed (more on this later), occasionally you have to write "The End" as you finish a writing session. Establishing hard deadlines may not work for all forms of writing, but it could help you stay honest to a production timeline.

The more engaged you are in your own writing though, the less likely you are to quit and the more likely you are to write every day, keep a schedule, and give yourself the freedom to write more when you are on a roll.

Don't Stop Believing

I could apologize for the cheesy song reference, and you can thank me for humming the Journey hit the rest of the day by buying one of my books. Or more than one, if you really love Journey or even just this one song.

This is important. There will be times in your life when no one around you believes in what you are doing. It will seem like no one understands you, and you will never make it as a writer. Tell them to shut up and keep writing.

Believing in yourself is an easy thing to say. It is much harder to do. There have been dark days, where I had little to no faith in who I was or what I was made to do. I have been where you are, and if you struggle with believing in yourself or acceptance, reach out to other writers. I promise no matter how seasoned or how great a writer seems to be, I assure you that person has struggled as well.

The being said, no one else will ever be as big of a fan of your work as you are: while you are your harshest critic, you are also your most intense motivator.

The point is to don't stop. Keep writing. Finish the project. Once you have mastered writing some words, built then maintained a writing habit, finish what you are working on. Only then will you be ready to move forward and actually do something with your writing.

But first, we are going to tackle one of the toughest and most unpopular topics in the production section of this book, writer's block.

CHAPTER THREE

A NOTE ON WRITER'S BLOCK

"DISCIPLINE ALLOWS MAGIC. To be a writer is to be the very best of assassins. You do not sit down and write every day to force the Muse to show up. You get into the habit of writing every day so that when she shows up, you have the maximum chance of catching her, bashing her on the head, and squeezing every last drop out of that bitch."

— Lili St. Crow

"Biting my truant pen, beating myself for spite:

"Fool!" said my muse to me, "look in thy heart, and write."

— Philip Sidney, Astrophel and Stella

So far in this book, you have been introduced to the basic parts of writing as a business and we have talked a bit about the first part, the production process. We've talked about the importance of writing some words and how to write more, faster. What about those times when the creativity just doesn't flow?

If you have heard me talk about writing at all, you have heard me say these words that seem to infuriate nearly every writer who hears them: I don't believe in writer's block.

I'll keep this chapter short because this is really a simple principle, I have shared dozens, if not hundreds, of times. The simple fact is this: by purchasing this book and reading along, you have at least entertained the idea of writing for a living.

You don't get to be blocked in the thing you do for a living. Remember when we talked earlier about writing every day, and we mentioned how you can't call yourself a server if you are not actually at work, serving people drinks or food, or both. A waiter does not get to have waiter's block, any more than a teacher can call in sick with teacher's block. It is about creative problem solving, a skill every worker uses to propel and excel themselves in their chosen career.

There is a basic toolkit each job has that you are able to pilfer from when presented with a barrier. Consider writer's block as one of those barriers to the production side of your job. At those times that you do feel stuck, you will be required to open the toolbox and pull out the right tool or tools to help you overcome what is challenging you.

Positive psychology asserts that barriers are opportunities awaiting a creative solution: They are presented to force you to meet an opportunity. The more creative and diverse your toolkit, the faster you are able to plow through them. Over time, you may even come to see getting stuck as one of the most inspirational parts of your production process – it will become the structures your most interesting work will be built upon.

In any other profession, if you are not able to work that day, you go home sick, your boss finds someone else who can do your job for you, or all of your work is waiting for you when you get back to the office, and you have to make it up.

The kicker is, you don't get paid, or you use sick time. But as a writer, you don't really have sick time unless you have set up a savings account just for that reason (which you should). If you don't work, you don't get paid.

No fairy comes behind you and does your work for you. It really is that simple. Does that mean there are not days when things are harder than others? Nope. Just like any other job, some days you feel it more than others, and some days are more productive. The thing that is most important is that you show up each and every day ready to work.

Trick Your Brain

You need to write every day. We covered that already, but what you are writing might vary. You may be writing a blog post, a technical article, or the next great American novel. You might even be editing your latest piece or working with an editor on a project.

One way to keep writer's block at bay is to trick your brain so it is ready for the work you are doing that day. Here is how it works for me:

- I use Scrivener for creative writing, short stories, novellas, and novels.
- I use Google docs for blog posts and some articles, depending on who I am writing them for.

- I edit fiction and write and edit non-fiction using Microsoft Word.

I never use Scrivener for editing, and rarely use Word for the initial creation of a fiction or even creative non-fiction work. Why?

When I open up each interface, my brain knows what kind of writing we are going to do. I don't have to stare at the blank page for long before my brain automatically goes into the proper writing mode. It's a trick. If I open Microsoft Word, my brain puts on my non-fiction writing or my editor hat, and I get more work done there.

You don't have to use these programs the same way I do, or even the same programs. The point is you should use the mechanics of the writing to trick your brain into stepping right into the appropriate writing mode.

Software is just one part of the equation. You can also write in different locations for different types of writing. Location could positively influence your production process. Going on a writing retreat where you have little to no internet access can be a productive way to get a lot of work in a short period of time.

You can use a different keyboard for each type of writing or create different logins on your computer. For instance, I could have a Troy Lambert login for my regular computer work, a Troy Lambert Fiction login with access to only certain programs and wi-fi turned off, and a Troy Lambert Non-Fiction for when I am writing blog posts or other technical writing where I might have internet access, but have certain sites like social media blocked.

All of these methods might seem a little extreme but stop for just a moment and think about the cost of writer's block, and the efforts you make to get to work every day. If your car breaks down, you take a bus, ride your bike, or find another ride. You must do the same for your writing work. Your mind can be one of your worst enemies or your greatest asset.

Write Something Else

Typically, a writer who writes for a living writes about more than one thing, has more than one project going on. This is because to write for a living, you usually need more than one stream of writing income. What this means for writer's block is if you are stuck on one project, you can switch and work on something else.

Can't get into the groove for the next scene in your novel? Write a blog post, article, or another short story. The point is when your butt is in the chair, and it is your scheduled time to write, you write.

Writing does not include emails, Tweets, Facebook posts, or a letter to your long-lost brother. It does include journals, plays, movie scripts, stories, articles, technical papers, ad copy, and dozens of other things, all of which could make you money.

From a blog post about digestive health to a brochure about your local furniture store, nearly every kind of writing you do involves creating a story of one kind or another. Sometimes you have to be creative to find what that story is. Usually for the writer, creating one story sparks another.

Also, don't discount your subconscious. While you are working on one thing, your brain may be working on another. The answer to your "block" on another piece of writing will often come to you while you are working on another. If you are writing, your brain is in the right mode, and the act of writing will help you push through.

Write Anyway

Even if you are stalled, and you only have one project or goal at the moment: to get the damn book/novel/story finished. If your brain will not let you get past this particular plot point, you still need to write during your writing time. How?

Go back and read the last bit of whatever you wrote and start writing anyway. Write gibberish at first if you have to. Your brain will kick in. Write another story about that character and how they got to this point in your book. Start to write about the weather, your breakfast, or whatever you need to accomplish today. Most importantly, just start stringing words together.

You can even write something ridiculous: "Suddenly, there was a giant explosion!" This might not make sense at all in a romance novel, but it may just get your mind flowing if you try to write from that point. Writing a thriller? Try "Suddenly Derek dropped his gun, turned, and kissed Steve hard on the lips." Maybe it won't work for your story, but often the ridiculous gets your brain moving. It also might launch you into a whole new genre, likely under a pen name.

If you have to, start typing the phrase "I will always write during my writing time" and keep typing it until other words come. They will. But you must write to activate the writer inside you.

There are no wasted words except for those that remain unwritten. You cannot edit an empty page or the thoughts that are locked away in your head.

A Note About Mental and Physical Illness

Writers are notoriously bad at taking care of themselves. A part of that is the sedentary nature of our work. We spend a lot of time sitting in front of a screen sometimes even in a chair that isn't the best suited for what we do. We stare at screens that are hard on our eyes, and all of these things can lead to physical issues that must be dealt with.

Also, studies show that for whatever reason, creatives are more prone to depression, anxiety, and other mental disorders including truly obsessive-compulsive disorders that are far from the joke they are often made out to be.

There are a lot of theories as to why, however if you are a writer with a mental illness, writer's block may not something you can just "snap out of." You may need to consider professional help or seek out support from other writers with a similar diagnosis. Psychological disorders should be taken seriously and demand some form of treatment or intervention.

For a long time, writers and those around them have been very dismissive of mental illness, and it has been difficult to come forward and ask for help. However, the writing community is very accepting of those who are different, and this includes those dealing with psychological problems. Even if the issues you are dealing with are just circumstantial or you have chronic and recurring mental illness, give yourself room to heal.

The same is true for physical limitations. Maybe you have a chronic physical illness, or you are diagnosed with cancer. Of course, this can affect your writing and even produce writer's block beyond what a typical writer encounter.

Up to this point we have talked about how writing is a business, and if it is your job you need to do it every single day. This statement is not to belittle those affected by mental and/or physical limitations. The point is to emphasize that if you need to take time off to take care of your mental or physical wellness, make this your priority. If you are ill, seek assistance and concentrate on your health.

Yet, don't let it block you indefinitely. Often writing is great therapy and can even help you heal in a number of ways.

Conclusion

You may have heard to become a proficient writer, you must put in 10,000 hours writing, or roughly one million words. Use your writing time to get some of the bad words out to make room for better ones. Do not ever, under any circumstances, waste your writing time.

If you are going to write for a living, you are not allowed to have writer's block. You need to work through it somehow. There are no sick days, and no one will come in the middle of the night and do your writing for you.

Whatever method you use to trick your brain, whether you write something else or just write anyway, you need to work when you are scheduled to work, and for those of us who are writers that means writing. Writer's block is a sick day, and you can only take so many of those before you go broke.

CHAPTER FOUR

THE REWRITING PROCESS

"WHEN YOUR STORY is ready for rewrite, cut it to the bone. Get rid of every ounce of excess fat. This is going to hurt; revising a story down to the bare essentials is always a little like murdering children, but it must be done."

—Stephen King

"The most beautiful things are those that madness prompts and reason writes."

—Andre Gide

Writing as a business is a complicated topic, and so far, we have covered several things, mostly related to writing, with brief notes on writer's block and how it is not allowed. There is another step we must cover before we move on.

There are a couple of things every author needs to know about editing: first there are several types and each editor calls them by different names. What it really comes down to is a process that has four main steps, although there can be other smaller steps under these.

They are, by the names I call them: developmental editing, content edits, line edits, and proofreading or copy editing.

And the first step, developmental editing, is one that publishers, in general, do not do. If your work is still in the developmental stage, they aren't going to accept it. Sometimes an agent will look at it if you are going a more traditional route for publishing, but they will not shop your manuscript around until it is out of this phase.

In fact, some authors going the traditional route will hire a free-lance editor do all of the above steps before they even show their work to an agent or publishing house editor. The reason? The more polished your manuscript, the more likely it is to get accepted, assuming of course that you had a good idea in the first place.

The good news is you don't always have to hire someone to do the first step, the developmental edit. Usually this step addresses issues in the manuscript you can deal with yourself or with a close group of friends or fellow writers who can help you perfect your craft. There are also books, programs, classes, and software that can help you address them.

Here is the kicker: if you are paying an editor, the more steps they do for you or walk you through, the more expensive their services are. It makes sense, right? The more work you do, the more you get paid. Editors do not, in general, work for free, although some may trade services with you if you do something for them in kind. Barter is often a mutually beneficial form of payment, but either way you are paying that person using either your money or your time.

What is the first step? It includes story development, re-writing, and revision. How much can you do yourself? Below we will touch on plot and structure, characterization, and dialog - which are part of story development - to be followed by common re-writing and revision practices.

Plot and Structure

Here is the deal. A doctor does not become a doctor by visiting a doctor, then thinking: "hey, I can do better than that" and opening a practice without the appropriate credentials from an accredited institution of higher education. Similarly so, you do not write good novels by reading novels and then assuming you can do better: Writers require some form of education along the way too.

The truth is, you may or may not be able to write better than the hack who wrote that book you just read, but you need to understand that, contrary to popular belief, there are rules when it comes to writing. You can break the rules when there is good reason to do so.

Rule breaking is an exception though. Most of the time, writers, like medical professionals, follow a formula to determine what is wrong the book they are working on. Writers also use a process to fix elements that are not working properly.

For a novel, short story, or any work of fiction, you must have certain elements for a plot to work no matter what genre you are writing.

The Inciting Incident: This is the point where the story starts. Everyday life was happening, and then something new and unexpected happens. That can be good (romance) or bad (thriller, horror), but it alters what is normal for your main character or characters in some way.

The Goal: Your main character must have something they need or want, and that is their goal. If you have a series of books, that is great, but the character in each book must have their own goal and must strive to reach it in that particular book. There can certainly be an overall plot for the series, and there should be, but each book must have goals that stand on their own.

The Obstacle: Something is standing in the way of your character reaching their goal or goals. This is usually the antagonist, but it can be a person, a place (some extremely difficult terrain), circumstances, (their arm is stuck in a crevasse when they are out rock climbing), or an emotional obstacle within themselves (fear, envy, or love). There can even be more than one obstacle, but one of them should be the primary barrier your character must overcome.

The Dark Moment: Also known from time to time as the "pit of despair". This is the moment when your character is at their lowest: all hope is lost, and it seems like they will be defeated and will never reach their goal. This moment creates the tension of the book and is the moment the reader should be most invested in the character.

The Big Idea: This is the turning point. The main character finds the one thing that could be used to turn their circumstances around to and achieve their goal.

The Resolution: We need to wrap up and answer the questions that have been asked earlier in the story. This is the point where the reader must feel things are resolved, at least for now. All the loose ends and hanging questions must be tied up. In the case of a series, you can leave some overarching questions unanswered, as long as you make it clear to the reader that more answers lie ahead, that your hero's journey is not over.

These things must also all occur with the right pacing. You will lose your reader if you slow down at the wrong places or speed up when they really want to see all the detail of a scene.

This is a really basic overview of plot structure, and you can discover more through books like *Story Engineering* or *Save the Cat Writes a Novel. Both books* outline two different yet very similar methods to structure your story and pace it correctly.

If your story does not have all of these elements, it is not done yet. You can pay an editor to point these things out for you and help you correct them in the developmental editing phase. However, with some education and time spent re-writing, you can learn to correct them yourself.

Characterization

This is the development of your characters, and this is something you can also learn and work on yourself. There are entire books on characterization and how to write the people in your story well.

The first place to start is by asking yourself a few simple questions about your character:

- **What is their primary strength?** What is the area where they are strongest, and therefore different from those around them? This can range from a superpower to simply being able to notice details no one else can. For example, in the case of the television show *Dexter*, his superpower was The Code his father taught him when it came to choosing who to kill. In *Breaking Bad*, Walt was a great chemist.
- **What is their greatest weakness?** Often the

character's greatest weakness is related to their greatest strength. Louis Lane, not kryptonite, is Superman's weakness, pride was Walt's in *Breaking Bad*, and The Code Dexter followed was often just as much a weakness as a strength.

- **Why should we care?** If your character has a weakness and a strength, but we do not care about them at all, it does not matter. We won't want to read about them. The key? We must know the story behind both their strength and their weakness, and we must be able to empathize with it. Inspiring empathy is a delicate matter and is an entire discussion of its own. It is essentially the writer's entire job. If the reader does not feel empathy for the characters and story, they will not be entertained, and won't keep reading.

Developing great characters is a part of the skill of any writer, and if you can do it well, especially in a first draft or in your second one, you will have a sure way to hook readers.

Dialogue

I encourage writers to read their work out loud whenever possible, or have it read to them using a program like Natural Reader or another speech to text program.

The reason is you can hear wrong wording and phrasing in your work you cannot "see." This allows you to fix it before you even send it to an editor. However, this is especially important with dialogue. You can hear how your characters sound when they speak and determine if they speak in a way that sounds organic while setting them apart. If they do not, it is time to revise your dialogue.

Writing dialogue is not easy, and again, this is an entire discussion of its own that can fill an entire book. Here are some simple tips to get you started:

- **Write dialogue at a coffee shop, or at least study it there.** You can have headphones in, so you do not look like a creeper, but listen to those around you. What words do they use and not use? How do they structure their sentences?
- **Don't copy the um's, ah's, and lengthy pauses.** Those do not translate well to writing (or to any form of fiction) but copy the overall style of natural conversation.
- **Use dialect and cute phrases sparingly.** First, they are hard to write and they distract the reader. Often in real conversation a dialect or accent is difficult to understand and results in a lot of "what?" and repeated sentences. **On the other hand,** cute phrasing tends to come off as cliché and when overused can feel tropey or stereotypic. Both cases just read horribly in a book, and you don't want your reader re-reading the last sentence and saying "what?". You want to pull them forward in the story.

Work on your dialogue. Insert emotion, senses, and other things that people add to their speech on a regular basis. Avoid the overuse of dialogue tags other than 'said' and cut every adverb possible. For example, don't use 'he said quickly'. And avoid things like 'she sighed' or 'he barked'.

There are other offending tags too, and it would do you well to read books like *Dynamic Dialogue: Letting Your Story Speak* by William Bernhardt. The other key is to practice writing dialogue, and let others critique your work.

The more quickly your dialog moves, the better it resonates within the story and the quicker a reader will plow through it. Lastly, the more understandable it is, the better for the reader.

Repeated Words and Phrases

You as a writer tend to repeat certain words and phrases. For a certain period of time, they become your favorites and you use them over and over. There are also common words that nearly every writer uses excessively or in the wrong places. When you are re-writing, search and destroy these words. Here is a partial list:

- That
- So
- Rather
- Very
- Little (as in a little hungry. Either he was hungry, or he wasn't)
- Pretty (as in pretty much, pretty small, pretty large)

Also search for commonly misused words, and make sure you are using them properly, such as their versus there versus they're and to versus too versus two.

The more you catch these things yourself the less your editor has to do, and the less you have to pay them. A simple method for finding them when you are re-writing is to search for them in your document. This often pulls you out of the story just enough to really look at the words rather than the rest of the prose around them. It also makes it easier for you to see errors and make corrections.

The Second Draft

The second draft involves you re-writing and clarifying your story.

It is not a full-on edit. It is simply fixing things like plot, pacing, characterization, and dialogue. You can help yourself by learning more through books, classes, writer's conferences, and other means, such as a critique group or enlisting beta readers (we will discuss these in the next chapter).

Here, really, is the point of this chapter: you should never show your first draft to an editor, agent, or most of the time to another human being. Most first drafts are crap, and they should be. As we discussed previously, you should write your first draft quickly, and often that means it won't be very good.

You must re-write. At the very least a second draft, but sometimes more. You need to revise, listen to your work, pay attention to plot, characterization, dialogue, and those words you repeat all the time.

Finally, once you have gone through this phase of the production process, you need to show your work to someone else. Every good work is created with a team, and now is the time to start reaching out to the professionals who will help you along the way.

But before we talk about that, we will talk about critique groups and beta readers and the role they can play in the production process along with the harm they can do.

CHAPTER FIVE

CRITIQUE GROUPS AND BETA READERS

"IT'S RATHER DISCONCERTING to sit around a table in a critique of someone else's work, only to realize that the antagonist in the story is none other than yourself, and no one present thinks you're a very likable character."

— Michelle Richmond

"Embrace the criticism. Take it to mind not to heart."

— Nate Hamon

"Writers are often the worst judges of what they have written."

— Stephen King, Everything's Eventual: 14 Dark Tales

Writer's groups, critique groups, and beta readers often raise large controversy in the professional writing community. Just bringing them up at BarCon—an unofficial event that happens after the day is over at every writers' convention—is almost a sure way to initiate a heated and impassioned discussion between writers.

The reason is simple. There can be a lot of good that comes out of writer's groups and even critique groups provided you have the right mix of people there. However, there are some simple ground rules everyone involved should follow that help to ensure positive experiences and beneficial outcomes. More on these general guidelines later in this chapter.

There can be some bad advice too. Almost every time an entire group of writers tell you there is something wrong in your work, they are right. On the flip side, when it comes to how to fix a problem with your work, they are, more often than not, wrong.

There are exceptions of course. I remember walking into a critique group knowing there was something wrong with the chapter I submitted, but not knowing what it was. One of the guys in the group, a fellow author, said: "What about doing it this way?"

That was exactly what I needed that night and at that place in my work. There were some requirements for me accepting it though. I needed to be open to hearing what he had to say, and we needed to have already established a mutual history with one another based on a high level of professional trust.

And that is the kicker in critique groups: you need a certain amount of trust. You also need certain rules in place to protect everyone's interests.

Below are some general guidelines. Before we begin, let me say there are plenty of exceptions to these rules, and groups that work on completely different ideas. The key is to find or create a group that works for you.

The Purpose of the Group

The purpose for some groups is encouragement. The purpose of other groups is to improve your writing. Know the difference going in. While both types of groups can be useful, the more you treat writing as a profession, the more you gravitate to groups geared toward helping you write better.

This may mean you have to leave a group geared toward encouragement and move to one that is more critique oriented. That being said, sometimes it is good to just socialize with other writers and talk about the awful and wonderful thing that is the writer's life. You might want to keep both groups as a part of your schedule, if you can.

The key is to know and understand the purpose of the group going in, so you don't hurt the feelings of others or get your own feelings hurt. Writing is hard enough without getting unsolicited critique.

At the same time, feedback can be extremely valuable and critical to your success. If you are in a critique group or interested in one, read on.

Respect and Putting Rank Aside

No matter how good you are or how experienced you are as a writer or how inexperienced you are, critique group is a place to put that aside. Sort of. You need to respect everyone in your group. However, there sometimes comes a point when that is not possible. We'll talk about that in a moment.

You need a mix of writing experience and expertise in a group. You need the great writers to bring everyone along to their level, but who also still need feedback on their own writing. Your group needs to be able to provide them with that feedback so they, too, get something out of the group.

You also need those who are less experienced. They often still think more like a reader than a writer, and that can be very useful for you and improving your writing skills.

Also, one of the best ways to learn something is to teach it. Meaning if you are one of the better writers in the group, you will improve and learn how to improve your own work by critiquing that of others.

Put Aside Explanations and Emotions

I always say you can be as artsy about your work while you are writing it, but if you intend to write for a living, eventually it is a product you need to sell. Feedback can be a huge part of making it better, but if you take it personally, it can also stop you in your tracks. When you walk into a critique group intended to help you improve your writing, you need to check your emotions at the door.

Also, you don't get to explain what you meant in a certain passage or by a certain thing. Many critique groups have the person being critiqued remain silent during the critique, but even if you can talk, stop and think about it for a moment. If part of your work is confusing enough to those in the group that they have to ask about it, you need to clarify that part for your reader. You can't go to everyone who bought your book and say, "I know this part is confusing, but let me tell you what I meant." It is better to hear this feedback in a critique group rather than in an Amazon review.

This does not mean everyone's feedback is created equal. This is the danger in critique groups, and what we will talk about in the next two sections. You can't write a book by committee, so you need to know what to submit to critique groups and how to evaluate the feedback you do get.

What to Submit

This is a good question, and it largely depends on the group and what you want to learn about your work. You can often even submit first drafts with the purpose of asking certain questions or receiving certain kinds of feedback.

For example, if you submit an unedited first draft, you are usually looking for story and character advice, continuity, etc. In this case, you aren't enlisting your group to correct punctuation or grammar. You just want to know if the general concept of your draft is working for the reader.

If your work is further along in the process, say a second draft, you may want validation that the idea is working however, you may also want some feedback on grammar, punctuation, spelling, and other common mistakes.

This also depends on the skills of those in your group. Some of them might be very good at catching story and character errors while others might be great Grammar Nazis. So, how do you know what to take for feedback and what to toss out?

Evaluating Feedback

Just like the real world, not every piece of advice you get on writing is good advice. In fact, you often get more value out of critiquing the work of others rather than from the feedback you get on your own work.

This aside, there will be those in your writing group who are really good at some forms of critique, and, over time, you will learn whose advice works and whose does not in any given circumstance. The key here is understanding and trusting yourself to decide which suggestions to take and which to throw away. If you blindly take all the advice you get, you will end up with a mess of a book.

Here are some things to look for:

- **Agreement:** If several people in the group say the same things about your work, look at it. There is probably some kind of issue there you should address.
- **Expertise:** Is the person sitting across from you a lawyer or legal aid for their day job, or were they once one? Take their advice on the legal aspects of your book and plot. The same can be said for ex-police officers, ex-soldiers, and others who have worked in specific professions.
- **Writing and Editing Experience:** Have a great editor in your group? Congratulations. You are one step ahead of many of them. Lean on the advice of experienced authors and editors when they alert you to issues with your work.
- **The Green-Eyed Monster:** Sometimes if you become successful, other writers will resent that success, and will tear down your work out of jealousy. If you have this problem in your group, you either need to talk to that person and resolve the issue, remove them from the group, or find another group better suited to where your career is headed.
- **Your Story:** Does the advice resonate with the story you are trying to tell? Does it make sense? Does this person just not understand your genre or ideas? Do others in the group disagree with them? Only you know your work fully and can judge whether the advice you get will work or not.
- **Petty Stuff:** Sometimes the advice you get will be about petty things: things that do not really matter to the

average reader and can be ignored. Don't make changes, especially in early drafts, to these petty things.

- **Bad Advice:** Sometimes those in your group will offer advice that is just bad. It will either derail your story or has little to no added value to what you are doing. It may even be wrong: incorrect grammar or punctuation or even poor plotting advice. Judge this by what those around you think of the advice. Sometimes you just have an instinct as a writer, and as you write more, it will get better. Learn when to listen to it and when to ignore it.

All of the constructs listed above, along with personality conflicts in addition to other interpersonal issues, are why some writers simply avoid writing groups altogether. In some cases, depending on the writers' groups available in your area, the downsides of critique groups far outweigh the benefits.

Beta-Readers

Once you are a couple of drafts in, and you have your work a little more polished, many authors work with beta readers. Beta-readers can be people you gift books to or even pay for the privilege of feedback. While they are usually not professional editors, they could be fellow writers or readers who read a lot in your genre.

The idea is to get feedback from actual readers before your book goes out into the world. They can often catch common mistakes you miss, point out things that just don't work for them, and give you some valuable insight into things you can do to make your work stronger.

The more professional you become, the more you will develop a fan base and the easier it will be for you to find beta readers. To begin cultivating beta readers, new writers typically borrow from other writers or enlist websites that promise to connect you with beta readers for your work.

Eventually, you will find those who give you the kind of feedback you need, respond quickly, and can be counted on to be honest.

Even writers who do not use writers' groups or critique groups usually use some sort of beta reader or early reader system to get feedback on their work before it goes to an editor and onto the other phases of the production process.

You will find nearly every writer has something: a critique partner or small group of them, a set of beta readers, or some system to get early feedback on their work. These groups and readers can be both good and bad, and what you get out of them largely depends on what you want and need from them.

Next we will talk briefly about self-editing, and how well you can really edit your own work.

CHAPTER SIX

A NOTE ON SELF EDITING

"BOOKS HAVE A PUBLISHING STANDARD, and every Indie Author is responsible to their readers in making sure those standards are met or exceeded."

— ***Eeva Lancaster,*** *Being Indie: A No Holds Barred, Self-Publishing Guide for Indie Authors*

We mentioned before that rewriting is not editing, nor is it self-editing. What do I mean by self-editing? This means editing your own work yourself with little or no input from professionals, and then sending it into the world that way. Even if you have the greatest critique group ever and the greatest beta readers, you still need professional editing.

The hard truth is if you don't use professionals to polish your work, it's probably going to suck, and there are a number of reasons for that. First, you are too close to your own work. You will keep things that should be cut, and you cut things that should be kept. Your editor and your beta readers help you determine those things.

They help you clear away the smoke, so the reader can see the fire you have built.

The second is you become word-blind to your own mistakes. There will be errors you will miss no matter how many times you go over your work. Your book will be riddled with grammatical errors, wrong word choices, misspellings, repeated words, and more. No matter how good a proofreading or grammar program you have, those mistakes will somehow survive.

Readers and reviewers hold your work to a ridiculous standard. If you took a test and got 99% on it, would you say you did well? This means in a 70,000-word manuscript you can have seven mistakes, and still be at 99.99% accuracy. However, most readers and reviewers will tolerate way fewer mistakes than .01% and may simply stop reading or leave a horrible review if you have more than three or four.

The key is to remember while there are several computer programs and people who can help you with revisions and re-writes, there is a distinct difference between what these programs can do for your work and the editing process. You may catch basic grammar and punctuation with them, but a good editor will go much deeper.

This means you need a team, at least one editor, one proofreader, and that's just the initial pass through. You will need to employ an editor and proofreader again after you have received feedback from the several early readers and critique partners you had enlisted to read your work. So please, don't self-edit. Ever.

For the sake of your career as a writer and your worth to readers, don't edit your own work. Rewrite, yes. It takes a village to raise a child, and it takes a great team to put out a great book. Doing it all on your own can only end in disaster.

CHAPTER SEVEN

HIRING AN EDITOR

"EDITING MIGHT BE A BLOODY TRADE, but knives aren't the exclusive property of butchers. Surgeons use them too."

- Blake Morrison

"No author dislikes to be edited as much as he dislikes not to be published."

- J. Russell Lynes

Here is the point where you are at the end of your free resources. It's time to bring in the professionals we talked about in the last chapter. You're going to need to hire several, and we will cover how to find and choose them, how to hire and pay them, and how to avoid common mistakes.

What makes me so much of an authority on this topic? I have been published by small presses and self-published. I know the work and expense that goes into both. Conversely, I work as a freelance editor and writer, and have worked with both. Over the last decade or so, I have become associated with literally hundreds of editors and writers.

There are many editors I would recommend wholeheartedly, and others I would not. I would also tell you, in the interest of fairness, that I am not the right editor for everyone. I am also very busy, as are many other freelance editors I have worked with. So, even if you wanted to hire me at any given time, my schedule and skills may not suit your needs.

Your Path to Publication

At this point in your writing process, you may not have decided yet what your chosen path to publication will be, but that only matters a little bit at this stage. Your work should be well edited before you send it to an agent, a small press editor, or a publishing house, especially if you are a first-time author.

As you go further in your journey, your publisher may be more inclined to accept an earlier draft, especially if you are on deadline, and help you walk through the editing process.

However, if you plan to self-publish, or if you are a new author or even new to a publisher, you should present them with your best work. This means you should find and hire an editor to help polish what you have created.

This comes after critique groups, re-writes, and advice from beta readers who are willing to read your work before it is published. As mentioned earlier in this book, these individuals should all be people that offer you valuable feedback, not just "I love it! You are so talented!" This is not the stage where you need cheerleaders: you need honest yet constructive critique.

A professional editor takes that to a new level. They have been trained on story and plot structure as well as grammar and spelling so they should be able to help you with word choice and many other aspects of your work.

The Editor Search

Once you have determined it is time for you to hire an editor, you have to find one. The search for an editor is much like a search for the right employee. There are some primary differences explained in the steps below.

Word of Mouth is the Best

Word of mouth is the best advertising for the editor, and it is also the best way for you to find one. Enlist other authors in your genre who are self-published and who have hired editors for the works they have published. You should do this by asking who they hired and what their experience was.

A good clue is if you have read their work: If you have seen glaring errors that got through the editing process, though it may not be the entire fault of the editor, it does offer a clue to how thorough the process was. It is something you need to consider when choosing an editor.

In self-publishing and even publishing with a small press, the editor is enlisted early in the process. It is important to mindful that anytime your manuscript is touched, typos and errors can occur: Even a copy editor, the author themselves, along with whomever is formatting the book for you can introduce them. (I have actually had an experience where this happened to me. That is another story for another time). This is one reason to follow the process I outline in this section of the book: it prevents, or at least minimizes, the chances of this happening.

That being said, if a book is plotted well, characterization is good, and the overall story is well developed it speaks to the talent of both the author and the editor who assisted them in shaping the story.

An editor can do damage just as easily as they can do good, so it is important to know the difference. If the author really struggled to connect with the editor, but the editor did a good job editing the book, it may be their individual personalities did not click. This is important to note as well: Liking and connecting with your editor will certainly make it easier to work together, but it is not essential to be able to work together. What is essential is that both parties approach the process in a mutually respectful and positive way.

Job Boards/LinkedIn

Having trouble finding an editor through word of mouth? You may want to look at job boards and LinkedIn. But these come with a caution: You should beware of any freelance editor who is not busy or is running ads to get clients unless for some reason they happen to have had a cancellation. There are certain job boards and internet forums to avoid, and that is one of the reasons I suggest LinkedIn. It is a place for professionals, and you are more likely to find a solid editor there who has a good reputation.

Job Boards: First, do not start with Fiverr or similar "cheap" or bargain job boards. If your first question for the editor is "how much will it cost?" you're starting the relationship on the wrong foot. As a part of running your authorship like a business, you should have budgeted adequately for an editor.

Later on in this chapter, we will cover vetting editors in more detail. However, while cost should be among some of the first questions you ask, it should not be your biggest concern.

Look for ratings and recommendations. They are very closely related to word of mouth in that you may not know the editor, but someone does, and that individual has had a positive experience with their brand and their services. These ratings and reviews will often give you a high-level, general picture of the editor, themselves, and their process.

I suggest that if you are shopping job boards, pick a few editors and put them in a to-contact list. Probably the first one you find will not be the one you settle on, but this will give you options, so you don't have to start searching from scratch.

LinkedIn: First, you should have a LinkedIn presence of some kind. As an author, it will help you a great deal, if in no other way than marketing yourself and a physical landing page for your brand.

Second, LinkedIn is a great place to make professional connections. These are not people who are going to necessarily buy your book. They are those who are going to help you make it into a finished product, distribute, and market it.

When looking for an editor on LinkedIn, use the search box to search for "freelance editor". If you just search the word "editor" you will get a lot of magazine and website editors and you may not want to wade through their profiles along with all of the legitimate book editors who will show up.

Establish a connection with them by "connecting". LinkedIn offers you several options when you do this, including the ability to send a message. Use language like "new author (or established author, if that is you) looking for a freelance editor for my [insert genre here] novel project".

This lets them know right away you are a potential client. Connections without messages on LinkedIn often result in requests for free work, something editors get a lot of (trust me, I do). While the editor will often accept your connection request, if your initial outreach is not professional and clear, you may never get a response from them at all.

Make a list of editors you have connected with on LinkedIn and then stay on that website. You are going to start the vetting process next, and their LinkedIn profiles will be your first step.

The Vetting Process

LinkedIn

Every professional editor will probably have a strong LinkedIn presence. Listed below are some simple things you can look for to let you know if you are dealing with someone experienced.

- **Look at Years of Experience:** Much of the time this will be under jobs: even if the editor has worked as a freelancer, they will list how long they have been editing professionally. If they have been doing so for at least three years, they probably have enough experience, provided they have worked in your genre, to make it worth your while to check them out.
- **Look at Education:** Most editors have a degree of some sort along with some form of ongoing education. If they are professional, they want to list classes they have taken and certificates they have earned to legitimize their qualifications.
- **Look at Recommendations:** One thing LinkedIn allows you to do is recommend someone who has done work for you. Editors will usually have some recommendations listed, although not always. Many authors tend to not have a strong LinkedIn presence, so don't know how to leave a review or a recommendation. Still, it is a good practice to look anyway.

- **Look at Endorsements:** While not all clients will write a recommendation, many will take the time to click on endorsements. If a significant number of the editor's LinkedIn contacts have endorsed them, at least you know they have a good reputation. This is especially so if they are also endorsed by their peers.
- **Look at Associations:** Just like other professions, including writing, editors have associations and professional organizations they are a part of, including local, regional, and national organizations. If the potential editor is connected to these groups, they are probably getting continuing education from various conferences and other sources.

Not all of these LinkedIn guidelines will apply to every editor, however you will now have a sense of their footprint and who they are as an editor, all by looking at their LinkedIn profile.

Website

The editor will probably have their own website, and usually it will be listed on their LinkedIn profile. It should offer some idea of what their editing process is, an overview of rates, and a clear way to contact them for more information or even hire them.

If their blog contains posts about editing, read them. Discover what they edit, what the process is, and what they think of the current state of publishing. Much of this will let you know if they are a good fit for you or not. If you do not share their views in some areas, working together could prove difficult.

Remember, just because an editor worked out well for someone else, or has a good website, or has a solid LinkedIn presence/profile, it does not mean they are right for everyone; this includes you.

Many editors will also include a calendar with their next openings for edits, although an equal number won't share that until you are further into the vetting process. If it is available, take a look. If the editor is booked up beyond the time when you want to have your book complete, you need to evaluate if they are worth adjusting your goals or timeline. If not, then you just need to move on to the next best fit on your editor list.

Other Social Media

While LinkedIn is a great place to gather information about a potential editor, you may also find that an individual's social media is an equally sound place to research certain qualities. What do they like and not like? What books do they read? What do they Tweet about? What do they do in their spare time?

Often if you can find other ways to connect to an editor outside of your writing, your professional relationship will be stronger. Trust will be built faster if you both share similar core values and visions about writing. An added bonus is you may find yourself developing a lasting friendship with your editor over time.

It is great that an editor is professional, but there will be times in the process of editing and publication when you will want to scream, cry, or just rant. Often, your editor can empathize and be a good sounding board. It's really about more than just editing your manuscript. It is about shaping your story and, in some ways, who you are as a writer. So, you should choose one carefully.

Meeting, and a Test Edit

Once you have selected an editor or group of editors, it is time to meet them. Whether that is in person or online, have them do a test edit.

Free Test Edits

Some editors offer a free test edit of a chapter or two to see how things go and to evaluate your writing. This helps them see how much work they are going to have to do on the rest of your manuscript.

It helps you see if you like their style, and whether they are a good fit for you. Obviously, free is the best price for a test edit, but be aware: This may not be as thorough as the editor will be once you are paying them.

Also, a test edit is only a small part of your book. There may be other parts that need more extensive work or less. Understand that there will be variations: if what you handed the editor is pretty polished, initial edits may not look as harsh as they will be where your work is rougher.

Paid Evaluations

The best of both worlds is to hire the editor, or more than one, to do a paid evaluation of your manuscript. They will look through the entire work then let you know what the problems are, what kind of edits you really need, and an estimate of how much it will cost to correct it.

Paid evaluations are better for both of you: the editor knows you are willing to invest in them and their opinion, and you know the editor has a stake in making your work a priority and will give it their best.

Making a Final Choice

There may be several factors that go into your final decision. Experience, education, personality, and of course that all important test edit or evaluation are important. No one can know the right editor for you other than you.

For example, maybe you chose someone with less experience than another editor. They had a good vibe, were potentially cheaper, and they offered you a great test edit. After all, how would they get more experience unless someone hires them?

This can often be a good move with benefits for both of you. You and the newer editor will learn from the process.

The flip side is that even an experienced editor, one who is really busy, may not be the best. They may have a limited time to work with your project, and if you have needs beyond the original scope of work they estimated, they may rush to finish your project, or even postpone part of the work to fit with their schedule.

This is why you must click with your editor, and you must be clear about expectations, what you'll do if things are not working, and how you'll move forward.

Once you have completed the vetting process, you will be ready to hire an editor. When you are ready, you will need a contract, one that has all the items above, and which you need to understand before you sign. We'll talk about that shortly, but first let's review the types of edits in more detail.

CHAPTER EIGHT

THE TYPES OF EDITS

"SO THE WRITER who breeds more words than he needs, is making a chore for the reader who reads."

— *Dr. Seuss*

"Edit your manuscript until your fingers bleed and you have memorized every last word. Then, when you are certain you are on the verge of insanity...edit one more time!"

— *CK Webb*

"While writing is like a joyful release, editing is a prison where the bars are my former intentions and the abusive warden my own neuroticism."

— *Tiffany Madison*

We touched on the types of edits briefly in Chapter Four when we talked about the rewriting process. However, this chapter lists more detail about each type we did not cover earlier. Remember, the simple rule is that the less an editor has to edit your work, the lower the costs. There is only so far in the editing process you can get by yourself, with your writing partners, with critique groups, and even with beta or early readers.

This is important. As stated previously, you will need to hire an editor. There is no way around it. However, you can present them with a pretty clean manuscript when you do, one that could potentially save yourself hundreds of dollars. Here is the breakdown.

Developmental Editing

You have a story, you have some words, but you really aren't sure at this point if everything is working. What is your plot arc? Are your characters deep enough or are they even likable? Is this enough of a story for a novel? Is there enough conflict? Too much? Is your story boring or is your story confusing?

The thing is, you can't really answer all of those questions on your own. The reason? You are too close to your own work and your own story. Of course, it is interesting to you. You know what you meant when you wrote it, so it cannot be confusing. That might not be true to someone else. Of course, the more experience you get as an author, the better you will become at detecting some of these nuances yourself, but you will continue to require professional guidance.

You can pay a developmental editor at this point. Usually, you pay by the hour, not by the word, because your manuscript is not defined enough yet for you to know how many words it will really have. A professional is able to assist you with story structure, characters, conflict, and any number of technical challenges you might be struggling with.

Given you are open to learning more about your craft, you could take care of much of this yourself. Here are some tips:

- **Join a critique group:** We discussed the good and bad of this previously, but it can offer valuable insight and be a wealth of assistance toward improving your writing.
- **Find accountability partners and small groups:** These are better than critique groups most of the time, as you can call these peers anytime and ask them about areas where you are stuck, different story points, and you are freer to meet anytime. Just be sure the people you enlist are actually helping to improve your writing.
- **Go to Conferences:** In other words, go to school. Take workshops. Learn from the masters. Every writer works differently, but the more tools you have in your toolbox, the better equipped you will be to solve problems on your own.
- **Read and study books:** A writer is always learning. *Million Dollar Outlines* by Dave Farland, *Story Engineering* by Larry Brooks, *Save the Cat* by Jessica Brody, and other books all talk about story structure and writing craft. Study and learn from them.

Not all of these strategies will work for you, and that is actually okay. Pick what does work. The point is you will save a ton on money if you are able to plow through the story development phase and the best way to do this is to enlist the help of peers, go to conferences, and research best practice aides and books.

If you don't have a group and cannot find one, hiring a developmental editor may be a great idea for you. Or maybe you are not getting what you want from your tribe of people, and you need more. Do whatever you have to do to make your story its best. This is a business after all, and the better the product you have to sell, the more successful you will be.

Content Editing

There is very little of this you can do yourself. Certain programs like Grammarly, Pro Writing Aid, and some of the plugins for Microsoft Word will certainly help, but often you will not see your own errors, and those in your friend group and even your peers will miss things. Remember when we talked about how few typos and errors readers and reviewers will tolerate? Without a professional editor at this point, those things will start to make their way through the process.

This is where word choice, grammar, sentence structure, and all of those things start to come in. Most of the time, an editor will do at least three stages of editing with you, and it will start with this one. This is also where the editor will catch errors in the plot or story. Did you leave something unresolved? Did you change character names in the middle of the story? Did your character's eyes start out blue and end up brown at some point? A pro will help you catch and fix these things.

Essentially, this stage is where the content of your book goes through the final shaping process. It is a really important step, and a good editor will make your story much better at this point. It should come back from them red and bleeding profusely.

Line Edits

In this stage, the editor will go through the manuscript line by line, making sure there are no words out of place, and everything makes sense. They will be looking for grammatical errors, sentence and paragraph structure, and more. They will also be looking for content errors that might have been introduced in the last stage. Typically, by this stage, you are not allowed to make any major changes to your manuscript.

The reason? Simple. Any additions you make then need to go through the content editing step again, which takes the editor more time. Since essentially you are paying for their time and skill, this only makes sense. Also, the temptation at this point is often to second guess your story and actually make changes that do more harm than good. Don't do it. That is what the content edit was for.

Copy Edits or Proofreading

Finally, the editor will make one more pass, a quick one, just looking for spelling, grammar, and other errors that might have gotten through. Once this stage is complete, you need to send your manuscript to another proofreader. By this time, your editor may also be word blind to certain errors, and a proofreader will catch those mistakes.

Think of it. By this time, you have had several sets of eyes on your manuscript: your critique group or partners if you have them, beta readers, editors, a proofreader, and maybe even more in your circle. Your team has been working with you on your manuscript.

Even with all of this editing and all of those eyes, there may still be mistakes that make it through. This is actually a part of what I ask another set of late beta readers, only a select few, to do at this point —let me know if there are errors. If they find them before your book goes either to the publisher or you are finally ready to hit publish yourself, you can save yourself a lot of embarrassment.

Now, before we move on any further, let's discuss editing contracts for a brief moment.

CHAPTER NINE

A NOTE ABOUT CONTRACTS

"A CONTRACT IS ONLY as good as the people signing it."

— *Jeffrey Fry*

"A professional who doesn't deliver as committed is not just lazy, he is a liar."

— *Amit Kalantri,* Wealth of Words

It scares some people that in many parts of the writing industry, artists and writers work without contracts or, essentially, without a legal safety net: You have paid someone to perform a service (or they have paid you) with no legal contract in place. This is not always as bad as it seems, because as the quote says above, a contract is only as good as those who signed it.

This said, for major expenditures like editing and, at times, graphic design, you need to have a legal agreement in place. The good news is, you might sort of have one and not be aware of it.

In certain states, an email thread can serve as a verbal contract, although it is harder to enforce than an actual legal document that is signed. The truth of the matter is, even if the person is someone you know, you should have a contract.

The reason is simple. Even if you don't take legal action, the person's reputation is on the line, and reputation is everything to a freelance editor, designer, or writer.

Friendships can be ruined, relationships ended or be damaged, or business' reputation could be destroyed due to lack of a contract. Here are a few simple reasons you need one:

- **Expectations:** It should be very clear to each party what is expected of them: what service exactly, will be performed and which tasks are included and not included in that service? What do you, as the author, have to provide them so they can perform those services?
- **Timelines:** How much time should the project take? Will it be done in stages, or is there a single deadline? What are valid reasons for deadlines not being met, and what are the consequences if they are not?
- **Payment:** How much will this cost, or is this an ongoing cost? How are payments to be made, and when? What forms of payment are acceptable?
- **Ending the Contract:** If things are not going well, how can either party get out of the contract? Is there a financial penalty?

These all amount to one thing: protection for both parties. The person providing the service knows what they will get paid and when. The person receiving the service knows what they will get in return for their money and when.

Instead of just talking about this in an ethereal way, let's take a look at a sample contract and go through the elements it should include.

Two Important Notes:

The first note is that I am not an attorney. I did have one help me draw up this contract originally, and it works well in my state for the services I contract out and perform. However, if your needs are different you should consult an attorney. Paying for an hour of their time can potentially save you thousands of dollars later.

Second, this is a contract for services you are receiving or providing. It is NOT a publishing contract. We will cover those later, but for the moment understand those are completely different, and require a whole different level of scrutiny.

For our example, we will use an editing contract for a book. This is the contract between the editor and the author. Let's get started:

Title: Freelance Editorial Agreement

The title of the contract immediately tells us what the contract is for and about. Underneath the title is a simple sentence that expounds on that definition:

"This agreement is between EDITOR NAME (hereafter referred to as Editor) and AUTHOR NAME (hereafter referred to as Author) and concerns the following manuscript:"

This of course can be modified to cover design, formatting, or even proofreading by simply changing the title and the job description in the first sentence. Manuscript can be changed to cover, or whatever the contractor is assigned to do.

In the case of a manuscript this is followed by three simple things:

- Author: The name of the author of the work, even if this contract is for a cover.
- Title or Working Title of the Work: This helps you when referencing the project in your communications.
- Length and description: How long is the book, what is the genre, and what other ways does it need to be defined? In the case of a cover contract, this is simply the type of covers needed: Print, Amazon, Barnes and Noble, etc. Be careful. Some cover designers charge more for each iteration. Know what you are a asking for before you start, and make sure it is included in their fees.

Tasks: In this case the agreement speaks of editorial tasks. It specifically speaks to different types of editing:

- Substantive and Structural Editing
- Stylistic Editing
- Copy Editing

These terms are defined on later in the contract, and this section explains that. This section may also include what the editor will not do, usually

- Scene rewrites
- Character profiles
- Additional writing

Sometimes this will include details specific to your case, or agreements you and your editor may have made ahead of time. In the case of tasks other than editing, this may include what the cover designer, formatter, or proofreader will and will not do.

For instance, a cover designer may be able to make banners and other items to go with your book cover, but those items may or may not be part of your agreement. Make sure the terms are clear, and you know how much additional work will cost.

Budget will be an important part of your project, especially when it comes to marketing, and marketing materials like graphics should be a part of that. We will discuss covers and marketing shortly, but, at this point, just know it is important to include your future needs in contracts you develop at the beginning of any process.

Delivery

This is an important section. How will you pass things back and forth? Will it be through Google Drive, One Drive, or some other file sharing service? Will you be working in a project management software like Asana? Will you be emailing things back and forth?

In most cases, you will be working virtually with someone who is not necessarily in your area, so hand delivery back and forth will not be possible, nor is it practical in most cases. This involves additional time, and usually causes the person providing the service to raise prices to compensate.

Payment

There are several options for online payments and invoicing. I use Square, PayPal, Bill.com, TransferWise, and even Square Cash. I almost never take checks as payment except from major publications who still pay that way, or some freelance and ghostwriting contracts where large sums of money are involved.

You and your editor, or other service provider should agree on one you both are familiar with and comfortable using. Make sure the amount of payment and timing of those payments is well defined, and that you include who pays any fees associated with that form of payment. Usually these are not large, but you need to include them in your budget.

Termination

This is where you define how the contract can be terminated by either party and why. Usually material change of circumstances or acts of God are acceptable. There should be a period of notice— usually between 10 and 30 days, and agreements of how much should be paid by each in the event of termination. Usually there is a financial penalty of some sort for the person who terminates the contract early.

For instance, if the author terminates the contract early, they must pay the editor for the work they have completed to that point plus a fee anywhere from $50-$100 dollars or more. Many editors are freelancers and may have turned down other work or planned their budget and time around a project.

By the same token, if the editor cancels the contract, they usually pay a penalty as well. The author will have to reset and find another editor, and this may cause them to miss deadlines. Whether those are self-created or a part of a publishing agreement, it is still important, especially if they have marketing release dates and events they may have to move.

Indemnity

This is important. Editing is a process of offering suggestions and advice. You as an author can take them or not take them, depending on how you want your story to be presented. The editor should bring questionable material to the author's attention, but they cannot read every work of fiction or non-fiction out there.

So, if you plagiarize something, or you don't change something the editor suggests and it results in a bad review, the editor is not liable for that, and you can't hold them legally or financially responsible.

This is to protect both of you, and at the same time to let you know that, while you do not have to adopt every change and editor suggests, you should certainly evaluate why they might be saying it.

Changes

This section defines how the contract can be modified, from deadlines to payments, etc. This can usually only be done by a signed addendum by both parties. This is simply to make sure you are on the same page, and there is no confusion about side agreements or changes you have made.

Terms

Finally, there should a be section that defines terms that have been used in the contract. This includes what copy-editing means, or what type of cover design will be provided. And what that means, or whatever other terms may be unclear.

If you have a question about an editor's contract, this is the time to ask for clarification, and not just verbally. It is not unusual for contracts to go back and forth several times for revisions until each party is happy.

Signatures and information

Typically, this is the place where each person signs and dates the agreement. In most states, you do not need to have this notarized for it to be legally binding, and hopefully you never have the issue anyway.

However, if you should, having a contract will make the process much easier. For the most part contracts are not used that way: they are simply used to create clarity to both parties.

What if you don't have a contract?

As mentioned above, in some states, a verbal agreement serves as a contract, and you can use it in court given you are able to prove the conversation happened. Even better is an email with a simple "I agree to create this item for this price" or "I agree to pay for this service at this price" is sufficient should you have to resort to litigation.

Terms and duties can also be clear from emails, so in the case of some smaller tasks a contract may be excessive. However, it never hurts to have one, and they really are not that hard to draw up and negotiate.

So, your book is done, you have hired an editor and have a contract in place. What next? What should you be doing in the production process while you are waiting for edits to come back? It's time for cover design.

CHAPTER TEN

SOURCING A BOOK COVER

"ASPIRING AUTHORS GET this through your head. Cover art serves one purpose, and one purpose only, to get potential customers interested long enough to pick up the book to read the back-cover blurb. In the internet age that means the thumb nail image needs to be interesting enough to click on. That's what covers are for."

— Larry Correia, author Monster Hunters Series

"Good cover design is not only about beauty... it's a visual sales pitch. It's your first contact with a potential reader. Your cover only has around 3 seconds to catch a browsing reader's attention. You want to stand out and make them pause and consider, and read the synopsis."

— Eeva Lancaster, Being Indie: A No Holds Barred, Self-Publishing Guide for Indie Authors

So far in this book we have covered a whole lot of ground. You have written the best book you can, revised it, and now you have hired an editor. Currently, they are working on one of the three to four rounds of editing your book will go through before a proofreader goes over it one last time.

If you are not writing your next book (you should be), you are sitting at home wondering what you should do next. The answer depends on your path to publication. If you are going the self-publishing route, it is time to source a cover by hiring a cover designer.

By the way, I don't care if you are a graphic designer and if you design covers for other people as a part of your business. You should never create your own book cover. I have known a few exceptions: that is, the rare occurrence that an author that could both write a book and create a cover for it, and sometimes it turns out okay.

Most of the time it doesn't. Your cover will come out very narcissistic and probably too busy. You will want to include too many elements of the story in one place rather than focusing on one central theme.

You should however know enough about cover design to know a good one when you see it. You should be knowledgeable about several design elements, and you should get second opinions about your cover before you give the artist the final yes.

The Bad

We will start with the bad, and sometimes funny, covers people have either created for their own books or had their four-year-old sister create for them using a box of crayons. A cover can be awful for a number of reasons: font, the photo, poor Photoshop skills, lack or relevance, wrong genre, or even horrible typos.

The problem is that a quick Google search will yield you hundreds of horrible examples. They are real, taken from Amazon and other sources. It's not just that they are bad, but that someone thought they were good, and good enough to publish. A part of the issue is that it is often hard to see the flaws in our own work.

Rather than just laughing though, focus on the different elements of a poorly done cover you have seen. Ask yourself what is wrong with them. Which elements are off? Is the font wrong? What about the photos used? Are they high quality? Cheap? Do they violate copyright laws? (more on that later in this chapter).

The Good

There are also some great book covers out there. The design is simple, the font is ideal, they stand out on a web page, the images fit the genre and are appropriate, and the words are spelled correctly: In short, there are no mistakes.

Look at the top 100 Amazon books in any genre. Chances are you will see some pretty good covers. What elements stand out? What fonts are used, and what emotions do they evoke from you? Do those emotions fit with the genre of the book?

In today's market, book covers must have some things in common, but they must be unique enough to stand out. You can buy a stock cover cheaply, but you might see another book with the same cover, just with the author and title changed. In fact, you might see several.

- Your title should be short, and accurately describe your story.
- The picture should be clear and simple, relating to one main element in your story.
- Your name should be legible and large enough to read.

Keep in mind that you are not the cover artist: you are the author. The cover artist is also a creative, so let them be. Come to the design process with maybe one or two things you would really like to see incorporated into the cover and let them do the rest of the work. After all, that is their job, not yours.

How do you find a good cover designer?

These answers are really like the ones regarding finding an editor. You simply need to employ a few additional yet simple steps:

- Find covers you like in your genre from self-published authors and ask them who they used. Word of mouth is still the best advertising, and the best way to find the help you need.
- Along a similar vein, find covers on books you like then read the acknowledgements. Authors often thank cover designers there.
- Search professional job boards or social media, such as LinkedIn. Avoid Fiverr or other cheap sites, just like we discussed in the chapter on editors. You get what you pay for when it comes to book covers, and too cheap to be true means you will lose on quality.

The search may take you some time. Look at sample work. Have the cover designer create a mockup for you, so you can determine if you like it or not. Just because a cover designer worked for one person does not mean they will work for you.

Remember, the cover is the first impression people will get of your book. Make sure it is a good one.

How much should I pay for a cover?

Okay, so here is the deal. If you are not paying at least $150 to

$200, you are probably getting an inferior cover. It takes at least a few hours for the most talented of book designers to work up a mockup or two, and then a few more to finalize the cover when they are done. They deserve to be paid for their time the same way you are when you go to work.

Most great covers are simple: like many other things in writing, keeping it simple is a much better idea, especially early in your writing career. Look at the original cover of the book *Jurassic Park* as an example.

If you are paying more than $1500, you are probably paying too much unless you are paying for a hand painted, specially created cover for a fantasy novel or something along those lines. If you do want that kind of cover, just understand a couple things first:

- Most books are purchased digitally now. It is unlikely your reader will be able to see or will notice tiny details.
- You must make money too. If you biggest expense is the cover, you may have a hard time breaking even, let alone making a profit.

Essentially, you should expect to pay between $150 and $1,000 for a good book cover. Anything outside of that range is because of special circumstances, and only you can decide if the tradeoffs on either side of the scale are worth it.

The Publisher's Choice

If you are traditionally published or published through a small press, they probably have their own cover designers. You will have to go with their choice, whether you like it or not.

However, some will give you the opportunity to have input on what your cover will look like. Take advantage of this but understand that the publisher will have the final say. You may get a few mockups and an opportunity to fine tune your vision, but the publisher is paying at this point (you pay them back later, in royalties).

Hire a Professional

I have used a few different cover designers through the years, and some have not been as good as others. Currently, I use Elle Rossi of Evernight Designs for many of my designs (including the cover of this book). Here are some ways to tell the professionals from the amateurs:

- Amateurs are on Fiverr and other cheap sites, desperately looking for work.
- Pros are busy most of the time.
- Amateurs do not have a portfolio, a website, or references.
- Pros have all the above, usually a portfolio hosted on a website, social media presence, and references they can give you.

A professional will offer you a quote, a mockup or two for you to choose from and elaborate on with the intent on working you until your idea is portrayed the way you want it.

Choosing a cover designer, like many other parts of the process, can be arduous and time consuming, and is a step that is essential for you to get right. The first impression your readers have of your book will be one created by someone else. It is your responsibility to make sure they get the right one.

Next, we will look at another part of production, formatting the interior of your book.

CHAPTER ELEVEN

DIY FORMATTING VS. HIRING A PROFESSIONAL

"GOOD DESIGN IS LIKE A REFRIGERATOR—WHEN it works, no one notices, but when it doesn't, it sure stinks."

—Irene Au

"The alternative to good design is always bad design. There is no such thing as no design."

—Adam Judge

We have covered a lot of ground in the production process. We talked about writing your book, revision and editing, the book cover, and now we are going to talk about interior design and formatting.

Don't think this is an easy subject: I used to and then talked to a bunch of writers at a conference. Although I tend to be tech savvy, and even report on tech developments as part of my freelance writing work, many writers are not.

In fact, some of those at the table were not familiar with many of the features of Microsoft Office, let alone the fact that there were other, better word processing programs for writers to use.

The truth is, many writers have difficulty with the more technical aspects of creating a book interior that can be uploaded to many sites in digital form. Even the directions for creating files suitable for Kindle or KDP Print templates can be challenging. For non-fiction authors, this may include adding extra features, tables, and photos.

If you are one of them, understand there is no shame in asking for help. You are not alone, and that is the reason there are many formatters out there, including fellow authors who do understand the process.

What are the pros and cons of learning to do your own formatting? Well, that, as many other things in the production process, depends on you and your ability.

DIY Formatting

There are several automated programs and templates on the internet that will help you format your book yourself. If you are writing fiction, have no photos or tables in your book, and want a simple eBook format, most of these will work for you.

The fonts will be simple and standard, although you can change them slightly, but your file will look good. Maybe not great, but good. If you have a Mac product there is a great program called Vellum that can actually be used to create some great interior book formats and files.

If you are accomplished with technology, familiar with Word,

Scrivener, or other programs this may work well for you, at least for eBook formatting.

However, if you are not good with those types of software, and have issues adapting to new programs, this may not be the answer for you, especially when it comes to print. Here are some definite don'ts when it comes to formatting.

Don't Trust Automated File Creation

Any program that promises to automatically create a beautiful Kindle file for you probably won't with a few exceptions. You need to check the file yourself once it has been created then proof it to make sure it works the way you want it to. This includes being especially attentive to the formatting at chapter breaks, parts, and other locations to ensure the breaks are occurring correctly, and that different types of fonts remain throughout the process.

Your files for fiction do not have to be fancy for the most part. In fact, I would argue that they should not be, at least for your eBook. But they do need to work efficiently on a variety of devices.

One of the best ways to ensure you have created a properly formatted book file is to follow the *Smashwords Style Guide* created by Mark Coker. Even if you do not publish on Smashwords, with only a few modifications of text (especially to the copyright page), this guide covers the most common mistakes, helping you create the best book file you can use to upload work for Kindle and other ereaders, or even to input into Vellum and other automatic file creation programs. We'll talk more about Smashwords and other distribution options when we get to that section of this book.

Never Create Your eBook File from Your Print File: Your print and eBook files should be completely different. The reason is that they are two different media. Print files are fixed where eBook files must be flexible. The user can change font type, font size, and may be reading on screens of different size.

If you try to create your eBook from your print file, it will probably look terrible. Beware! I can tell a few pages into a book if an author has done this due to funky spacing and pagination issues. Most of the time, I will not finish reading the book and rapidly abandon it.

If you do not know what you are doing or have questions around whether what you're doing is effective at all, STOP. Hire someone. Don't risk a reader's first impression of your book be that you did not even take the time to format it professionally.

The second thing a reader sees after the cover is your interior formatting. Make sure it leaves them with a good impression.

Hiring a Professional Formatter

This is much like the process of hiring a cover designer: look for a formatter by word of mouth, ask for references, and look up their work. See if what they do matches what you want your book interior to look like.

Let the formatter do their job though. Just because you want something in your eBook format doesn't mean it is possible or practical. Listen to the professional and let their experience guide you.

Remember when we discussed cover design? The cover designer is an artist, and to a lesser extent so is the formatter. The reason you are hiring a professional is that they see things you do not, and you have determined you cannot do the work yourself. Trust them.

Also, don't ask the formatter to teach you how to do what they do yourself, so you won't need them next time. That is like going to a restaurant and asking the chef to teach you the recipe for the dish you ordered.

First, they are too busy to teach you how they prepared your food. Second, they are teaching themselves out of work. It is inherently disrespectful to do this, and many formatters will openly let you know they don't appreciate it. Others will just never work for you again.

Additional Notes on Print Formatting

eBook formatting is one thing, print formatting is another. Sometimes chapter and title headings can be really eye catching, there are certain fonts you should not use, and adding even small images and drop caps at the beginning of each chapter can really set your book apart.

These things do not work for every book, though. If your chapters often start with dialogue or short paragraphs, drop caps may not work for you. If you are writing non-fiction, the interior of the book can be even more complex; so can templates. There are also rules for what page chapters should start on (always the right) and how certain parts should be formatted.

You can learn these, but a pro will know them already. If you can do this, and do it well, great. It is a skill that can be learned. What is important to note is whether this is a valuable way to spend your time: Meaning, you should weight the cost-benefit between hiring a professional or attempting to do your own formatting: It may be more cost-effective to farm this so you may concentrate on your talents on what will make you money: your writing.

The Value of Your Writing Time

We will talk more about this as we go forward in this book, but the most valuable way you can use your time is usually writing. Working on your next book, and the next one, in addition to other writing that helps boost your platform as a writer is where the bulk of your effort should go. Your brand should be a top priority for you.

Sometimes, hiring a professional to do this process is one of the best ways to free up time for writing. Remember, most celebrated chefs have sous chefs who do much of the prep work for them, and they seldom, if ever, prepare the actual dishes that come to the table. It's not that those tasks are not important, but the chef has more important duties.

If you are traditionally published or published with a small press, they will handle this step for you, and you may or may not have any say in what the interior looks like. Fortunately for you, they typically hire pros to do this work, and your interior will look good by default. If it does not, you do have the right as an author to say something and try to have them fix it. Remember, you want your book to look good, and ensure it is something you are proud to distribute and market.

We are nearing the end of the things you need to do for the production process, but before we go any further, it is time to take a look at publishing contracts.

CHAPTER TWELVE

A QUICK NOTE ON TRADITIONAL PUBLISHING BOOK CONTRACTS

WRITERS CAN WRITE whatever they want, but after THE END, when they self-publish their book, they become accountable to readers for the quality of the book they're selling."

— *Eeva Lancaster,* Being Indie: A No Holds Barred, Self-Publishing Guide for Indie Authors

"Sometimes wandering the indirect path is exactly what's required to get where we need to go."

— S.K. Quinn

Obviously, if you are self-published, you will deal much more with the contracts we talked about earlier. These are the ones where you hire someone else to do work for you, such as editing, a book cover, and formatting. The other tasks you might outsource, including marketing, we will discuss later.

However, if you are published traditionally or, like me, are a hybrid author who has both been published traditionally and self-published, you will deal with book contracts in addition to other types of contracts as well.

As before, I will preface this chapter by saying that I am not an attorney, and you should get one to at least look at your book contracts to ensure they are fair to both parties: You should understand the terms of the contract and be comfortable with the terms offered in them. In this chapter, we will just briefly look at some key terms you should be looking for, and why they matter.

Defining Traditional Publishers

For the sake of the discussion in this book, we are going to lump two very different types of publishers into one group. We are going to blend small presses and the Big 5. The reason is that we are taking a general view of contracts, and we aren't going to get too deep.

In most cases, I would not recommend the Big 5 publishing route for most authors unless you have an agent and already have a large author platform to sell from. In today's market, the name of the publisher does not matter as much as your name and reputation.

Small presses and even medium presses generally have more writer-facing terms in their contracts and will give you more personalized attention. For now, just understand that traditional means a publisher publishes your work, while self-publishing means that you do it yourself.

Keep it Simple

First, a book contract should be simple above all else. There are only a few things you need to cover, and that should be all that is in the contract. Publishers work to protect their interests and their revenue, and you should work to keep yours as well. This means that in reality the main points of the contract consist of a few simple items:

- **Pay:** How much of the net profits do you get for each print and eBook sale? This is your royalty.
- **Rights:** What exactly is the publisher buying from you? Which formats? For how long?
- **Decisions:** What decisions do they make for you about your books and what decisions do you make? What do you have a say in (covers, editing, distribution, etc.)? Usually the publisher will have the final word in these areas.
- **Marketing:** What is the publisher responsible for, and what are you expected to do? Who pays the cost, or do you split it?

Let's look at each point in more detail and address some key constructs to look for.

Pay or Royalties

Many authors self-publish because of this one thing, however, in large part, this is because they lack a fundamental understanding about royalties. Below is the skinny plus my advice, but to be frank, you should do your own research.

Modern publishing is a pay now or pay later proposition. Either way, you are going to pay for certain things. For instance, we talked about sourcing an editor, book cover designer, and formatter. If you recruit them yourself, you pay them yourself, and that means you outlay the funds ahead of time, expecting to make them back in royalties.

If a publisher contracts your book, they pay for these things for you now, and expect that your book will sell enough copies that they will earn those costs back and more, allowing them to make a profit. The publisher will keep some of your royalties, but you get a contracted percentage of them.

In this way, you are paying them back for what they spent up front on your book. You are still paying but the upfront costs are deferred. You will need to sell a certain number of books for the publisher to break even. Equally so, you need to sell a certain number of books before you break even if you pay for those things yourself.

The thing is that every contract has a different percentage attached to royalties for each type of book sold. Print pays lower royalties, because the books cost more to produce, so the net profit is smaller on each copy sold, percentage wise. Also, you usually don't sell as many print books as you do eBooks, at least in the case of fiction sales.

With a non-fiction book, you tend to sell more print books; this is closer to an even split. People often want a physical copy they mark up, highlight, and bookmark in order to refer back to. Although you can mark up an eBooks, print books still have a huge foothold in non-fiction; so, it is important you are getting the percentages you should from print book sales.

eBooks on the other hand are another story. You produce them once, and other than marketing, there are few ongoing expenses. This means royalties are higher and should be. eBooks are almost passive income to both you and the publisher, as long as the eBook continues to sell. Continued sales in this format depend more on our final discussion category, marketing.

What percentage is okay to accept? For print books, percentages are often low, even under 10%, but for eBooks, the Authors' Guild has established that half of net proceeds is an equitable number. If you are at 40%, that is not bad. If your publisher is offering 35% or lower of eBook net proceeds for your royalty, you should probably look elsewhere or try to renegotiate the contract.

Do your research and go with your gut. If it sounds wrong, seems too good to be true, or simply feels off somehow, enlist your attorney, and talk to other authors. Don't be afraid to say no and find another publisher elsewhere.

Rights

The most common rights are North American Serial Rights. If you don't understand these, a simple Google search will enlighten you enough to know the basics. However, there are other rights you must look at in each contract, because they can make a huge difference in your earnings besides dictating what you write next. Below is a short, high-level list of rights to be aware of:

First Right of Refusal

This simply means that if you write something in the same series or sometimes even in the same genre, the publisher has the first right to look at it before you offer it to another publisher or publish it yourself. Read this part carefully: writer careers have been stalled or even destroyed on this contract phrase. Never underestimate the legal means of your publisher; they will pursue legal action if you choose to violate this section of the contract.

Movie and TV Rights

Not every publishing contract mentions these rights, but most do. What this means is that if your book or story was optioned for television or film, your publisher, first, has to authorize the deal, and secondly, they get a cut of the money.

This can be a good thing. Publishers often have resources and knowledge in this area you don't, and because they are getting a percentage, it is in their best interest to get you the best deal possible. However, if you have a small publisher, this might not be the case, and in fact might work against you.

Ask questions about this section, especially if you are even thinking about a screenplay or other production options. Your publisher could get rich off of your hard work if you fail to negotiate this properly.

Audio Book Rights

Audio books are becoming a more popular medium at the moment, and if you want to produce one, you will have to go through your publisher to do so if they own these rights. This may mean you have little say in the narration or production process. You, typically, aren't able to do it on your own unless you buy these rights from your publisher.

Often acquiring these rights can be as expensive as the rest of the process. Talk to your publisher about offering your work in an audio format to determine what their plans are. If they have no plans for an audio book, and you want to have one for your work, ask to keep these rights at contract time rather than renegotiating for the rights later.

Make sure the audio book rights include the right to use the same cover in addition to other marketing images so that the book brand remains consistent. Questions? Again, an attorney is well worth the investment for any special circumstances.

Other

There are other rights related to the book cover images, certain marketing images, and even what you can do with your name, especially if you use a pen name. If you work in a certain series, the restrictions may be even greater when you go outside the series.

Again, read carefully. For any questions about rights, ask an attorney and get them figured out ahead of time before you sign anything.

Decisions

This is a rather general category, but it has to be. Sometimes these things are under rights or under other sections of the contract. They may or may not matter to you but looking at them, at the very least, is important. Here are some questions that might come up that you should be able to answer.

What about the book cover?

Many publishers give you no choice at all in this area, others give you a couple of choices to approve from. Know ahead of time what your options are, and, notably, what your contract says happens if you totally hate your cover or cover designer.

What about the editor?

Sometimes, personalities clash when going through the editing process, or you just don't like what the editor is doing to your manuscript. What happens in this case? In some instances, you are just stuck with the editor the publisher chose, and you don't have any options but to grin and bear it. Others may offer you the option to switch one time as long as all deadlines are met. Still others offer some sort of mediation in the case of an author-editor disagreement.

To Print or not to Print?

Many publishers now are digital first presses. If your book earns out, or allows them to break even, and then starts to make a profit, it will come out in print. If not, it will be an eBook until it does make a profit, but often, in these cases, there is a time limit on when the book must earn out in order to go to print.

The same principle will sometimes apply to audio books as well. If your book sells in one format, the publisher will consider putting it in other formats. It is that simple. However, you cannot break from the contract and print on your own or make your own audio book. The publisher owns those rights, and unless you purchase these rights or otherwise obtain them from the publisher, you, as the author, do not have the legal authority to do so. This is why the rights section is so important. Pay close attention to what you want before you sign-off on this part of the contract.

Other

Again, do you want something special from your story? Do you want something unique in your book interior? Remember, the story is yours, but technically you are contracting with the publisher to create the book, which is theirs. They can give you as little or as much say in the process as they want or as you are able to negotiate.

Still, remember what we said in earlier chapters about the cover designer, the formatter, and the editor. They are professionals at what they do. Trust them with your story and your craft. Resist the urge to micromanage them. Whether you hire them, or a publisher does, they are part of a team that has making your story the best it can be a part of their vested interest.

Conclusion

Here's the bottom line. Book contracts are complicated. The bigger and better the deal seems, the more likely it is that you need an attorney to at least look over the contract. At the same time, you need to know the basic terms and parts so that you don't sign-off on an inequitable deal.

Poor contracts, rights of refusal, and the wrong publisher have cost authors thousands of dollars and hundreds of hours of work. Many careers can be made or broken by these contracts. Read, understand, consult, and ask questions. Protect yourself, your work, and your career before you sign any contract with any publisher.

CHAPTER THIRTEEN

THE PROOF

"I WAS WORKING on the proof of one of my poems all the morning, and took out a comma. In the afternoon I put it back again."

— *Oscar Wilde*

One of the final things that will happen when you write a book is that you will get a proof. Usually, proofs come in the form of a PDF for print or occasionally as an actual printed book, and you will get another proof for the eBook. Even if you are self-published, you should be creating and checking your own eBook proofs, and whoever you print your books through, be that Ingram, Amazon, a private printshop, or all of the above, you should get a print proof before you print any number of copies.

By this point, you have been wrestling with this book for a while now. You have written, rewritten, been through the editing process with an editor, the proofreading process with a proofreader, worked out creating a cover, and either formatted the book or had someone format it for you. You have seen it over and over again, read it a bunch of times, and now you have (hopefully) moved on to writing something else.

In short, you feel done with this book. And here comes one final look at it. You might be tempted to skim or not look as closely as you did the first time or the fourth. Resist the temptation. Study the proof. It is your last chance to make any corrections. Don't blow it.

Typos, Spelling, and Grammar

You would think by this point that every typo that could be caught will have been, but you would be wrong. Typos may have been introduced in the editing, proofreading, or formatting process. Have the same beta readers who read the book originally look at it again. Hunt down and kill every typo and spelling error you can. Run it through a spell-checker and grammar checker one more time but look at every word yourself too. You need this copy to be clean, because this is the final step before publication.

I stress here, this is your last shot at fixing any grammar and punctuation errors. You may be shocked at what has made it through the rest of the process. Fix everything you find that might be wrong at this point. Double check if you have any question and ask someone on your team if you are not sure.

Formatting Errors

One more time: make sure you did not make any mistakes with formatting. Does your book look good inside and out? If it does not, now is the time to get things straight. Everyone wants to put out the best book they can, and every one of us makes mistakes. Take your time. Look at every single page with a reader's eye. Is there something that distracts you? It will probably distract a reader too.

What the Proof is Not

This is not your shot at making major revisions. Probably your page count is pretty set along with the table of contents: major changes at this point will move create a trickle-down effect of even more changes to the work's format. Unless you find something really major, the book is done. It is now time to let it move on. Rewritten pages and paragraphs will mess up the formatting. Any new material will have to be edited and proofed. You will be starting part of the process over again.

If you are with a publisher, they won't tolerate any major edits at this point. If you are self-published, you shouldn't either. You are on to the next project, so keep moving. This one is done, so it is time to stop playing with it and get it published. You can't sell a product until it is complete, and the proof is the last step to finishing it.

At this point, you, as a professional, should have a release date and actively marketing it (more on marketing in the final section of this book). Pushing it back will hurt both sales and your reputation. This is especially true if you are self-publishing. If you are going to be successful you will be held to a higher standard professionally than those who are more traditionally published. Your reputation will mostly be tied to what you have done lately, so your most recent performance will matter most.

When it comes to deadlines, self-imposed or those set by a publisher, meeting them shows your commitment. Missing them shows you are just an amateur. Part of setting yourself apart is your commitment to writing for a living means you hold yourself to a higher standard as well.

CONCLUSION: MOVING FORWARD

YOU HAVE COMPLETED the production process. You have written a good book, had it edited and proofed, then finalized the words that will be inside. You have even formatted them correctly or hired a professional to complete the formatting for you.

You have a great cover and have looked over a print and digital proof. You've done everything you could to ensure you have the best book possible before hitting the publish button or, if being traditionally published, giving your publisher the go-ahead to publish your book.

Is it done? No. A book is never really done according to its author. You could revisit and re-write it over and over. What would be the point of that? Eventually, what are you doing to the book will make it worse, not better.

Besides, you need to be working on the next book, and the next one. Every book will get better.

The art part of your work is over. It is now time to move on to the business part. You came, you created, and that is great, but you now need to proceed to selling the product you have created.

The first step in doing that is to get your book into places where people can discover it. That means everywhere from your own website to Amazon and other digital distributors, bookstores, and even libraries.

How do you take what you have created and do that? We are going to tackle that in part two of this book, Distribution.

PART TWO

DISTRIBUTION

"Despite the promise of four days of sun and overly sweet wine, Richard was sporting a sour puss. But then that was to be expected - he sold books for a living, after all."

— *Charlie Hill,* Books

Unfortunately, the distribution part of the writing as a business is generally considered less fun than the production part by most authors. We would all like to sit in an ivory tower and write books to distribute to the masses who just happen to be waiting in anticipation for our next collection of words and ideas.

This isn't the way things work. We will talk about marketing in the final part of this book, but in this part, we will focus on the distribution piece. Because before you market your work, you must make it available to the masses somehow. It needs to exist in a variety of formats. If a person learns of your book but cannot find it, that does you no good. You can't sell it to someone you can't get it to.

I encountered this recently when trying to find a book for a gift. The book was not available in the US at all, print or otherwise. I had to order it from an overseas vendor, and it took over two weeks to arrive. The reason was that this particular author objects to the United States political situation in a number of ways and has made the decision to not offer his latest books here.

While it does make a political statement, if I had not wanted that particular book so badly, I would not have sought it out, and the sale would never have happened. The author, and his publisher, are missing out on a large number of sales in the United States as a result. Since the author is from the UK and sells more books there, the impact may not be as great as it would for others, but the point is the limited distribution of the book not only made a difference in whether I could find it or not, but also impacted the difficulty I had in getting it.

Of course, when it comes to book distribution there are a ton of choices. We will examine them in order over the next few chapters.

- Amazon Exclusivity vs. Wide Distribution
- Wide Distribution Options
- The Risk of Pirates and Plagiarists
- Print Distribution Options
- Audio Books
- New Trends and Future Options

All of these have their own level of importance depending on your book, your genre, and what your marketing plan is.

A note here: for those who are traditionally published, usually your publisher will make the decisions about distribution for you and will tell you where your book will be available and if you will have audio books or other options. This does not mean you should skip this next section. On the contrary, it means you should be knowledgeable about distribution so you can be an informed participant during the contract and the publication process. Regardless of who does the distribution, you should know where to send people when they look for your work online.

As stated here, the distribution of your book can make the difference between it being found or not being found by your readers. A part of writing as a business is being familiar enough with every aspect of the publishing industry that you know if something is wrong.

If you think that there is a place your book should be found, you need to encourage (and sometimes incentivize) your publisher to get it there.

Let's explore the different kinds of distribution and the pros and cons of each. This will set us up for the final part of writing as a business and a word almost every author dreads hearing: Marketing.

CHAPTER FOURTEEN

AMAZON EXCLUSIVITY VS. WIDE DISTRIBUTION

"SCOTT AND FRANKLIN did a terrific job of articulating exactly what we've stood for throughout our many disagreements with Amazon, namely, that a diverse literary marketplace is a healthy literary marketplace. And I'm personally encouraged— though not surprised—that so many readers agree."

--Roxana Robinson, Authors Guild President, 2015

Smashwords challenged the publishing industry when Mark Coker launched it in 2007. By 2010, the company was profitable and distributing books not only on its own website, but through partnerships with Apple, Barnes and Noble, Kobo, and Sony.

Apple, while partnering with Smashwords, was also in the self-publishing game, and Amazon offered Kindle Direct Publishing options to authors starting in 2007. Apple was the first to offer authors a 70% royalty under certain conditions and Amazon KDP soon followed. Compared to traditional deals which often offered print royalties from 4-7% to new authors, this was a big deal.

Then Amazon, as per their usual mode of operation, started Kindle Select. This platform requires that authors offer titles exclusively on Amazon in exchange for certain benefits: marketing options are one of them, including the ability to run 5 free days of promotion and 7-day Kindle countdown deals. The books in the exclusive program are also offered in the Kindle Unlimited program, a program where readers pay a certain amount each month to read as many books as they would like, similar to a Netflix subscription.

The payout from Kindle Unlimited varies quite a bit from author to author, as they get paid according to a "pages read" formula based on a monthly global fund set by Amazon. Many authors find great success with this program: many think it damages author earnings overall.

This sparked controversy among self-published authors: Do you distribute your book as widely as possible, making it available on several different platforms? Which ones matter the most? Should an author use something like Smashwords, Draft2Digital, another service, or should one upload their work to each outlet directly?

Alternatively, is it better to deal with Amazon exclusively and offer your book only to Kindle and Kindle Unlimited readers? We'll tackle each of these in turn and examine the costs and benefits of each method.

Wide Distribution

It sounds like a great idea: Getting your work in front of as many people as possible seems like the logical answer, and for many authors it is. The reality is that most author sales come from Amazon: they are the largest book distributor in the world.

However, number two is iBooks through Apple. Many authors are also finding success selling books on their own website and directly to readers through Smashwords, Draft2Digital, and other platforms.

For the majority of this chapter, we will be talking primarily about eBooks, since they are the bread and butter of most fiction writers at the moment. Print books are more expensive, harder to distribute, and you make less money from each copy. However, having them as an option is great, and as we mentioned before, are essential for any non-fiction author.

Smashwords

There are, of course, several ways to get your work on all of these platforms. One of them mentioned already, and one of the oldest platforms is Smashwords. Smashwords was formed by Mark Coker after he and his wife shopped around a manuscript, made all of the changes requested by publishing houses, only to have it still be rejected. They knew they had a fan base; they just needed a way to reach them.

Mark went to work in 2005 on developing his own distribution site and launched it in 2007. It is still one of the largest eBook distribution platforms in the world. Smashwords also helps writers distribute their work to retailers like Kobo, Barnes and Noble, iBooks, and library and subscription systems in exchange for a small royalty.

They used to also distribute books to Amazon KDP, until Amazon changed their ability to do so, and created a more exclusive platform. More on that in a moment. Smashwords is unique in a number of ways. They were the first to offer eBook distribution in an affordable way. Mark has written several books, and through them offers tons of free advice from how to successfully format and upload your eBook to marketing and other advice for authors.

Smashwords Alternatives

Of course, Smashwords was not the only company to form an aggregate for distributing books. Draft2Digital, Lulu, and other self-publishing platforms soon followed Smashwords. Ingram Spark is another, and many of these have one primary advantage over Smashwords as they offer print on demand services as well.

Individual Uploads

The other option you have for wide distribution is to upload your books to all of the different outlets where you want it placed one at a time. There are pros and cons to this option.

Pro: You'll get the highest royalty from each. Smashwords and any other book distributor takes a percentage of your sales to cover their costs of placing the books for you. This is usually a percentage or royalty rather than being a flat fee.

This means the more books you sell, the more they make, which can be a good thing, as they will help you market your work. However, this also means less money in your pocket at the end of the day.

Pro: Your book will be in exactly the right format for each platform. Every eBook format and platform has its quirks. If you do individual uploads, you can be sure that your work meets the requirements for every site and distributor.

Pro: Some platforms, like Kobo, offer ads to those who upload their work directly. This is an option they do not offer to those who publish on their site through affiliates. These ads are often very effective.

Con: It's time consuming and can be complicated.
Just as knowing your book will be right for each platform due to
each one's quirks, you will have to deal with those quirks when
uploading files. Don't get me wrong, once you have done it a few
times, it does become easier. However, there is still a time cost
involved, and you need to factor that into your schedule and your
business plan.

Pros: Better metadata. If you upload on individual platforms, you are able to collect better search metadata on each,
making your book easier to discover on that platform. This metadata also translates to Google and other search engines when
potential readers are looking for your work. More discoverable
work sells more and earns more money.

Advantages of Wide Distribution

The advantage of distributing your book widely is that those who
do not use Amazon for whatever reason can find your book in a
number of places. These can include digital library collections.
eBook platforms are popular in other countries, and there are those
who use iBooks and Apple products exclusively.

While Amazon is number one in book distribution, the second
distributor is iBooks. Depending the genre of your work and how
well you reach desired markets, you could be missing a large
segment of customers if you neglect having your work distributed
on iBooks and on Kobo.

However, some research shows that while not everyone uses
Amazon, many people who use iBooks and Kobo also use Kindle
apps to purchase books that are exclusive to Amazon. We'll discuss
this option next.

It is simply important to understand that wide distribution means
you may reach a larger variety of readers. You never know when

one of those readers will become a "superfan" and spread the word about your books far and wide.

Missing even one reader could be potentially costly. So, why would anyone want to distribute exclusively through Amazon? There are some valid reasons, and we will talk about those next.

Amazon Exclusivity

After reading the above section, you may wonder why anyone would choose to distribute exclusively anywhere. The reason is simple: Amazon offers some unique benefits for authors who do so.

What are those unique benefits, and why do they matter? Here is a quick overview.

KDP Select

Kindle Direct Publishing is the platform authors use to load their work on to Amazon, and it is abbreviated KDP. KDP Select is the program by which authors offer their product only through Amazon for a period of at least 90 days. In exchange, authors receive certain privileges other authors and most publishers who do wide distribution do not.

Free Days: You can offer your book for a certain number of days in each 90-day period. Offering a book for free, especially if you have a series or other books for readers to find, has the potential of boosting rankings and sales over the long run. This includes the book you offer for free or your other work.

You can also offer Kindle Countdown Deals: These are deals where your book starts at one price and changes over the course of a few days. These are easy deals to market and coupled with good social media and Amazon ads could net respectable short-term sales in addition to long-term exposure.

Your books will also be automatically enrolled in Kindle Unlimited, Amazon's Netflix-like book lending program whereby readers pay a monthly fee and read as many books as they would like.

Kindle Unlimited

I'm treating this as a separate topic, because some authors love it, some hate it, and there are very few in between. The way it works is this: every month, Amazon sets a global fund for authors whose work is in Kindle Unlimited. The author gets paid according to the number of pages read by those who subscribe to the program.

As with any system like this, there have been those who have cheated it by having bots read books for them, hiring click farms in India and other countries where "readers' click through books quickly to get tons of page reads.

Amazon cracked down on this, but unfortunately many legitimate authors who were not cheating also got in trouble when they had sudden uptakes in pages read. This only added fuel to the controversy.

Many authors argue that this system is hurting author incomes rather than helping them. Authors who are well-known get more page reads and make more money. Those who are able to work the system continue to take money away from the fund, lowering the amount available for other authors.

Others claim Kindle Unlimited payments have boosted their income and hail the program as an innovative way for authors to earn more. The system seems similar to Spotify or Apple Music. For some, the rewards will be great: for those who do not have pages read or "listens" as in the case of musicians, the system will feel broken.

Either way, Kindle Unlimited is an option avid readers love, and authors are divided on. Amazon calls it a benefit for authors in the KDP Select program, and it can be, with proper marketing support.

Conclusion

Wide distribution verses Amazon exclusives has been a debate for several years now. Amazon proponents like Hugh Howey will tell you that this "all my eggs in one basket" approach works, because at any time an author can move their eggs should they become dissatisfied.

Others say this is foolish: missing readers on other platforms is simply not worth the price, even if the benefits are legitimate.

Ultimately the answer is up to you: do you want your work many places, or can you make an Amazon exclusive work for you?

Personally, I am an author who advocates for wide distribution most of the time. There are a few exceptions where exclusivity works for an author, but they are rare. As a result, the focus of the next chapter will be on wide distribution.

CHAPTER FIFTEEN

WIDE DISTRIBUTION EXPANDED

"LIFE WITHOUT A KINDLE is like life without a library nearby."

— *Franz McLaren*, Home Lost

"Growing up in the digital age, I'm expected to embrace all forms of modern technology with blissful ignorance. Books were always one of few escapes from this, because reading a book means not having to look at another damned glowing screen - which is why, no matter how "convenient" or "enhanced" digital enthusiasts claim that eBooks are, I'll never see them as real books. They're just files of binary data, and while they might be considered books by a large amount of people, eBooks have lost the human quality that real books have. You can argue that this is pretentious or stupid or nostalgic, but ultimately what will you pass down to your children and grandchildren? A broken old Kindle device with the same files that millions of other people have, or the dog-eared paperbacks that you fell in love with and wrote your name in and got signed by the

author and flipped through in the bookstore and kept with you for years, like an old friend?"

— *Rebecca McNutt*

Now that we have talked about the Amazon exclusive versus wide distribution options, we need to talk about the options besides Amazon. What do we mean, exactly by wide distribution? How do you get your books on all of those different channels including print? It sounds like a daunting task, and it can be.

But there are those who will never find your books any other way. Wide distribution is the answer for most authors. Although there are some shortcuts, to do it right takes time and energy.

First, there are services that will actually do some of the work for you. Services like Smashwords, Draft2Digital, or Pronoun are called aggregate publishing platforms, and they will assist with the distribution of your eBooks either for a fee or a percentage of royalties.

There are also people who will help you do this. Instead of getting a royalty, like an aggregate site, you pay them a one-time fee to put your books on those sites.

They key to these aggregate platforms is they are much like having a publisher: they take a percentage of your royalties or charge a fee for distribution, which means you make less money than if you did all that distribution work yourself. At the same time, you don't have to do all of that distribution work. Like many other parts of the publishing industry, it is a matter of putting your time and effort into the places that help you make the most money.

You can publish your book to the individual platforms as well. We talked briefly about Amazon already, but here are the others (in no particular order).

Apple iBooks

Apple is the second largest eBook platform in the US market. The Apple platform, however, could stand some improvements.

The reason is simply this. As with other Apple initiatives that have fallen off the radar of top management, iBooks, while it has some cool features for creating enhanced books, has languished. Apple is known for being the best in many areas, and in this one they fall short.

Outside of using an aggregate, uploading books to the iBooks Author platform can be a bit tricky, and is something that will take time for you to master. While many authors get good results from iBooks, it is a small percentage compared to Amazon.

Still, if you are going to distribute widely, iBooks is almost a must. You will need to have an Apple ID, connect that ID to iBooks author, and upload a properly formatted ePub edition of your book.

There are tons of tutorials out there, and once you have mastered the process it will go fairly smoothly.

Barnes and Noble

The bad news is this: The Nook itself and Barnes and Noble eBooks are decreasing in popularity, and it appears, at any moment, the entire division could disappear. Of course, so could Barnes and Noble, whose attempt to compete with Amazon have met with constant obstacles as it struggles to navigate the big-box, brick and mortar world of publishing.

Does this mean you should not publish on Barnes and Noble? Of course not. It just means that while Nook still has a faithful, but small following, you may wake up one day to see that your books, and everyone else's, have disappeared from Barnes and Noble virtual shelves. One could easily envision how this could occur given the recent closure of the Nook Forums online.

This said, uploading is pretty easy overall, but like iBooks, the process can seem painful the first few times. It can be mastered, or, again, completed through an aggregate.

Distribution success utilizing this platform is varied and subjective: I have known some authors who have had decent sales success through Barnes and Noble, while others who have had so few sales, they have given up on the platform altogether.

Kobo

If Barnes and Noble is in the sunset of their business lifecycle, Kobo is in a pretty good spot. In Europe and Canada, Kobo has a large presence.

Publishing on Kobo is, therefore, well worth pursuing. One of the advantages of self-publishing in the digital world is that your audience is worldwide, not limited to your town, your state, or even your country.

Once you have created a Kobo account, publishing directly with them is pretty easy. Your book can be uploaded as a .doc or .docx file then Kobo will handle the conversion process: You could also choose to upload an ePub yourself.

You can preview how the file will look on Kobo once you have uploaded it if you have an online ePub reader.

Depending on your genre and your marketing efforts, you may expect to receive a large number of sales on Kobo, certainly enough to make this relatively simple upload process worthwhile. An added benefit of developing an international following is that it could help boost Amazon sales and sales on other platforms.

Overdrive for Libraries

The Easiest way to get your eBook onto overdrive and available to libraries is by using an aggregate. The issue for Overdrive with most authors is the marketing piece of this: simply because your work is available to libraries does not mean they will actually carry it. Library budgets are small, and the ones for digital books are even smaller.

The other debate is ownership. While a library can buy your print book if they wish, when they "buy" your eBooks, they are only getting the rights to use them in a specific way. Therefore, unlike print books, the library is not fulfilling one of its primary missions: preservation.

Still, if you are able to encourage enough people to request your books, a library will carry them. If you are selling enough books, this may happen organically.

Either way, if you are distributing widely, you should find a way to offer your book on Overdrive, even if you don't end up making a lot of money from them.

The library dynamic is changing. Overdrive is offering new pricing models that make it easier for libraries to offer more eBooks. Don't neglect this important area in your distribution, and again in your marketing further down the road.

Your Own Website

Of course, the place you will make the most profit from selling your books is to sell them on your own website. There are a couple of ways to do this as well. You can either set up an ecommerce site and sell the book files and print books to readers directly, or you can set up a file distribution program like Gumroad or SendOwl. They take a fee for each sale, but they will provide support in case anything goes wrong with a download.

If you don't use a service like this, you take responsibility if anything goes wrong, and you also ship any print books ordered yourself. This is not necessarily a bad thing, but it does mean some more work on your part.

For digital files, I prefer to use a service, while for physical books, you will probably sell numbers you can handle from your own site and do your own shipping.

The big plus is you keep all the profits rather than just a 70% royalty, and you absolutely control that distribution platform. No one can take it away from you.

Others

The list of other sites where you may distribute your book is huge and could go on for days. In fact, you could spend days uploading your books to all of them (another argument for using an aggregator) only to get few or no sales from some of the lesser known markets.

There are additional subscription services popping up all the time, similar to Kindle Unlimited but for a wider audience. These sites are a great place to be, best reached through an aggregate like Draft2Digital, and often can result in some unexpected sales numbers.

However, you never know when one sale will lead to another, and you will develop a new audience. Many authors take the chance on these smaller markets for that reason alone. Honestly, it is not a bad strategy, if you are able to upload easily and quickly.

As we mentioned earlier, for many wide distribution is the best answer. Besides, once you are distributing widely, you might as well go all the way.

Look, anyone who pretends to tell you they have all of the answers to the distribution puzzle is probably lying through their teeth. What works for one author will not always work for you, and even if it works once for you, it may not continue to work the same way the next time. The publishing world is constantly changing, and you need to keep up if you are going to treat your writing as a business.

In this section we just talked about digital distribution. There are other forms to talk about, including print, audio books, and other emerging technologies and ideas, like subscriptions and more.

Before we move on to talking about those, we're going to talk about the risk of piracy involved with wide distribution and aggregate sites, and what you may want to do (if anything) to combat it.

CHAPTER SIXTEEN

PIRATES AND PLAGIARISTS

"PIRACY IS ROBBERY WITH VIOLENCE, often segueing into murder, rape and kidnapping. It is one of the most frightening crimes in the world. Using the same term to describe a twelve-year-old swapping music with friends, even thousands of songs, is evidence of a loss of perspective so astounding that it invites and deserves the derision it receives."

— *Nick Harkaway,* The Blind Giant

"Deep down, people who deliberately distribute other people's music and stuff feel contempt for professionals. And it's not just culture — these days lots of people are contemptuous of everything. Without realizing it, they're searching for things to despise."

— *Fuminori Nakamura,* Evil and the Mask

And it's probably about five, ten percent of the people who actually discovered an author who's their favorite author, who is the person who they buy everything of [by buying the book]. They were lent it.

They were given it. They did not pay for it, and that's how they found their favorite author. And I thought, "You know, that's really all [piracy] is. It's people lending books. And you can't look on that as a loss of sale. It's not a lost sale, nobody who would have bought your book is not buying it because they can find it for free."

What you're actually doing is advertising. You're reaching more people, you're raising awareness. Understanding that gave me a whole new idea of the shape of copyright and of what the web was doing. Because the biggest thing the web is doing is allowing people to hear things. Allowing people to read things. Allowing people to see things that they would never have otherwise seen. And I think, basically, that's an incredibly good thing."

— Neil Gaiman

One of the problems authors face is that of pirates and plagiarists. In some ways, this is a backhanded compliment. As Neil Gaiman says, if your work is good enough to steal, congratulations. With nearly half a million books published annually, that is saying something. Many of them will never be widely read, let alone pirated.

Pirate sites comes in many forms, but most of the time they offer one format or another of your book for a discounted price or even sometimes for free if readers will subscribe to their site or email list. This usually involves a fee of some sort. Essentially, they have stolen your work, and are selling it without paying you any royalties.

Many of these sites are not that successful, and you will note that there are few to no downloads of your books. This is in part because readers will find your work legitimately unless you are a very large name, but he pirates gain a following by promising a certain number of titles available. In recent years, the problem has risen with books that are in a series. When readers Google the next book in your series, these sites have often built up enough authority and ranking with Google that they appear right next to Amazon and other legitimate sites. Most often, the thief gets your book in one format or another from an aggregate and performs a conversion.

Readers are often fooled by these sites and buy your books there or even download them for free. This results in lost revenue to authors and publishers and hurts the industry overall. So, what can really be done about it?

Here are some common facts and ways to handle pirates.

To DRM or not to DRM?

DRM, if you do not already know, stands for digital rights management. What this does is protects your book so that only authorized copies can be read on the devices they are downloaded to. DRM also makes it difficult to transfer books from one device to another even for those who legitimately purchase your work.

Enabling this feature may seem like a good idea, but it does inhibit some readers from using your work the way they would like to. For instance, if I backup the Kindle files from my Kindle to my computer and reload them onto another Kindle, the files with DRM enabled will sometimes no longer work, and I either have to go re-download them or I can't access them at all unless I purchase the work again.

For families who want to share books, this is also a problem. However, there is also another side to DRM. It is incredibly easy to remove from a file, leaving it unprotected. In other words, DRM pretty much protects you from honest people, and often aggravates those who would otherwise read your work, but it does nothing to stop pirates other than slowing them down for a few seconds.

Aggregates that we have talked about like Smashwords and others often do not apply DRM to their files, and this is often where pirates get your work. They purchase an unprotected file in the form of a PDF or another format that is easy to convert; they then they copy it, and they now have your book in a format they can sell or give away. Either way, you are not getting paid for your hard work.

DRM is not as popular as it once was, but many authors still opt for it hoping it will slow the rate of piracy. Ultimately, it is not incredibly effective at preventing the practice. The choice, of course, is yours.

DMCA Takedown Notices

Legally, as the copyright holder of your work, you have the right to send a DMCA takedown notice to any site that displays your work for sale or for free, and they have to remove it or face criminal action. Once they receive a DMCA, most owners remove content almost immediately. Typically, your books are not worth the risk of legal trouble.

If you want to recover potential damages from the site, you will need to enlist a lawyer and sue. For most of us, this would not be worthwhile. The reason is that you have to prove the economic impact the infringement had on you. In other words, you have to show lost sales that correspond with that sites download or purchase numbers. If the difference is 10 copies a day, even times a month, the recovery settlement even if you win would be less than the cost of your legal fees by quite a magnitude.

Copyright Law

Technically, you own the copyright to your work as soon as you create it on your computer. Those files are time stamped, and you can often prove ownership of your work that way. However, that may not be enough, especially in the case of plagiarism or extreme piracy. What then?

Well, you could copyright your books more formally, and it is actually a good idea and well worth the cost for most authors. The reason? Your legal rights will be legitimized under the law and, as such, your legal rights will be easier to defend in court should that become necessary. This is especially true due to some recent changes in copyright law.

The need for such litigation is rare, but they do happen. To protect yourself to the fullest, contact the Federal Copyright office. There are a few different options for obtaining a copyright to your work, and usually the simplest and least expensive ones work well for books.

In the book itself, you are required to have a copyright page that states the date your book was published and who owns those rights, you or a publisher. It needs to state that all rights are reserved and that your book cannot be copied for any reason. You should have a clause that says it can be quoted for the purpose of reviews or other promotion, but that other uses require your permission.

Of course, this is a quick section on copyright. There are a lot of ins and outs, and if you don't already have a lawyer you are able to consult with, get one. Learn all you can about copyright law, how it affects authors, and follow your legal counsels advice when it comes to your work.

Your Time Wasted

As you may have gathered from where we started, writing as a business is a busy life. You could spend a great deal of time searching for pirated versions your books and sending out DMCA notices.

The reality of that situation is this: you probably won't find many pirating sites. Even if you do, they will have little to no impact on your sales because of how these sites rank in search engines. If you are doing things right, they will be far below your Amazon page, your social media pages, and your own website.

In other words, your time spent hunting down these sites and sending out notices that will not yield you any significant revenue. In fact, it will probably cost you valuable time you could spend doing something else, such as writing your next book.

Time Savers

This does not mean that you should not chase down pirates at all. It means you can save yourself a lot of time and effort with a few simple steps.

- Set up Google Alerts for your name and the name of each of your books. If you don't know how to do this, Google it: it's pretty easy. Google Alerts enables you to see when you or your work appears in search engines. You could then determine if the mention is legitimate or not. If it looks like a pirate site, you may verify it before sending a DMCA.
- Check Less Frequently. You can check once a month and still be okay. Set this time aside on a day when you are already doing other administrative tasks, so you will not be interrupting productive writing time.
- Have a DMCA template (there are plenty available on the internet) and modify it for each situation. Don't rewrite a new one every time.

- Don't sweat the small stuff. Many of these sites come and go quickly and have little impact on your sales and income. Leave these little sites alone unless you have the time to pursue each one. They'll disappear anyway. Focus on big sites that are actually selling your work and that of other authors.
- Enlist the help of other authors. The likelihood is that other authors are on these sites too. The more DMCA notices they get, the quicker these sites shut down. Reach out to fellow authors, encourage them to search their work on that site, and issue DMCA notices of their own.

This does bring up another note: only the owner of the copyright or the publisher can issue a DMCA. You can't send one for someone else, and someone else can't send one for you.

Pick your Battles

Here is the primary point. There will be pirates as long as there are eBooks. There will be a need for DMCA notices and policing but pick your battles. Don't waste too much time on this. You need to be working on your next book, on marketing, or other tasks. If you have an assistant or someone who helps you with your administrative work, this can be part of the tasks you assign to them.

Is All Advertising Good?

We're going to talk about marketing in just a little while, but you could think of piracy almost as advertising. Likely no one who is going to legitimately buy your book will knowingly go to a pirate site to find it anyway. This said, pirated books are available widely and could actually enhancing the reach of your work and your name.

If someone lends your book to a friend, or they check it out from the library, it is a way for you to be discovered, but you are not getting paid for that either. Fighting piracy is sometimes worthwhile, but often instead you can just leave it alone. Keep writing, keep working, and distribute your books through wide channels legally, and pirates will probably have little to no effect on your overall income.

Now that we have talked about the effects of piracy and what to do about it, we can move on to truly wide distribution information, formats besides eBooks. Next, we will talk a little about the role of print books and that method of distribution.

CHAPTER SEVENTEEN

PRINT BOOKS

"EBOOKS ARE THE NEW PAPERBACK. For genre fiction, they are the disposable counterparts to the paperbacks we used to buy."

--Troy Lambert

Books are no more threatened by Kindle than stairs by elevators."

--Steven Fry

We should be delighted people still want to read, be it on a Kindle or Nook or whatever the latest device is.

--J.K. Rowling

One of the oldest forms of book distribution is print. Since before the printing press when stories were written down by hand and books were transcribed over many generations, print has been the way many people digest books. Enter the last couple of decades.

The ereader has grown in popularity from dedicated reading devices to apps on other devices, even our phones. Which is better?

The answer is neither. Both have their place, and you need to decide for your books and your genre what that place is. How do you do that? Well, it is actually pretty easy. First, let's break things down a little.

As we mentioned in the contract section, there are several digital first publishers, ones who publish all titles digitally at first, and then publish print if they sell enough copies in one format. Why is this?

Because eBooks are the new paperbacks. They are the books that we grab if we want to read something but having a physical copy on the shelf we can read, highlight in, and refer back to is not important. This must be qualified by saying this principle applies primarily to genre fiction.

There is a trend though in textbooks and other academic works to move toward eBooks if nothing more than the lower cost and how easy eBooks are to update compared to their print counterparts. Still, print has a solid place in non-fiction and research materials, although that may be change over time.

Sales

For my first novel in my first trilogy, *Redemption* I have some amazing data that still holds true several years after its initial publication. Though it has been historically one of my bestselling books, I have sold approximately 1,000 eBooks for every one print copy sold.

While these numbers may not be typical, they are close. There are many mid-list authors who never print their books at all, but instead only sell them digitally and are very successful at it. So, why print at all?

Because as a self-published author, you make pretty good money on print books percentage wise. Secondly, and perhaps most importantly, they are a great marketing tool. Even if a reader does not buy the physical book at a signing, downloads almost always go up after those events because people go online and purchase the digital version of your book.

I often say that print books are very expensive business cards, and in some ways this is true. They are walking billboard ads that inspire others to buy your book. Print books get your name out there in ways digital books cannot.

Think of a person reading a book on an airplane or in the airport. If they are reading on a Kindle or other device, no one knows what they are reading. If they are reading a physical book, the cover is right there, as is your name.

If you are a non-fiction author though, this same principle does not hold true. You will probably sell about half eBooks, half physical, although your numbers may vary, in part depending on your marketing plan and your marketing efforts.

Depending on what you write about, print books can also lead to speaking gigs and other opportunities for "back of the room" book sales. These can be a great way to make money and further build your brand's prestige and reach.

In addition, local indie bookstores are a very good place to sell print books in that it is a mutually beneficial growth opportunity for both you and them. We'll talk more about indie bookstores specifically in another chapter but suffice it to say they are an essential part of writing as a business to authors. Besides, the indie bookstore is a great way to reach out and be part of your community.

The Ego Thing

There is something special about holding your first book and even the ones after that in your hands in physical form. It helps you feel success as an author; makes you feel legitimate. This feeling of confidence is something many writers need.

This is not without cost though. If someone does not like your book or your cover, you could become discouraged too. Writer egos are large but fragile things, so be careful that ego is not the only reason you want your book in print.

The Cost

Print books are an ongoing cost when it comes to production. There are two options to explore: print on demand or doing an actual print run. Doing an actual print run will result in a lower cost per book than print on demand, but you are typically taking a risk and ordering more books at one time. This can be a good thing: it incentivizes you to sell them rather than have them sitting in your garage. More on that in the marketing section of this book.

If you are working with a publisher, they will set a price for author copies of your book, and usually the difference is significantly lower than what you can sell them for in person. This means you usually, published traditionally or self-published, will make a higher amount and percentage on your print books than on eBooks, even though you will sell fewer of them if you sell them yourself.

However, the ongoing cost is not the only one. You will need an expanded cover for your print book because it will wrap and cover the spine as well, and you will need a blurb and probably an author bio for the back cover. This is usually not a big deal for your cover designer to do, but it does involve some additional expense.

Additionally, you will need to format your book for the print interior. Your eBook format is a simple design designed to respond to different ereaders and screen sizes. Your print book will need to be a static interior with certain types of formatting (depending on the type of book). You will want to explore font options, chapter headings, page numbering, and a table of contents that contains chapter titles (if you have them) and numbers.

These things will all cost you money to set up. In fact, many digital first publishers will not put your book into print until it has sold a certain number of digital copies. This is largely due to this additional setup cost.

The other factor is that your profit margin will be even lower if someone buys your book from a bookstore. Usually on a $15-$20 book, this can be as low as $1-2 per copy. Sounds minuscule, but it can easily add up.

So, why do print at all? With some genre fiction, many self-published authors never do. There are benefits though, so be sure to keep reading before you make the decision.

The Benefits of Print

There are some key benefits to print books, and while these are in some ways changing, they still remain relevant at the time of this writing.

- **Expanded Distribution:** Print gives you options for more distribution in libraries and bookstores. Print gives you the option, but it is not automatic. You have to contact both bookstores and libraries to get your books placed there, and even then, they may not accept them.

- **Discoverability:** If you do get your print books in libraries or bookstores, people can discover them by simply looking on the shelves. Also, if your book is in more formats, you have a bigger digital footprint on Google. The more places they are available, the better. More on that in the marketing section coming up.

- **In-Person Events:** It is difficult to sell digital books at in person events. It is much easier to sign books and hand them out. Also, if people see your physical books, it may inspire them to order your digital ones. Your physical books become a visibility tool, essentially an expensive business card or billboard of sorts.

These are all great reasons for print, but there are more.

Marketing

We will talk about this more in the final part of this book, but everything you do with distribution should have a purpose, and that purpose should be to promote the sale of books and to promote your name to a broader, diverse audience.

The more you do this, the better it will be for your writing as a business overall. Print books are in places you cannot be and are there when you cannot be there. The library is just one of those places and bookstores are another.

So, should you create print books? In some cases, the answer is yes, in others the answer is no. It depends on your goal for the book itself, and how much benefit you see to having it in print. Also, it depends on the length of the book. Putting a novella in print is usually not worth the expense and effort unless you bundle a couple of them together into a collection.

When we arrive at the section on marketing, we will also discuss the importance of how you publish your print book if you are self-published. It will make a big difference on not only how widely you are able to distribute your book and how much work you have to do to make it happen: This will make a difference in who will give you shelf space for your book.

CHAPTER EIGHTEEN

AUDIOBOOKS

WHEN YOU READ A BOOK, the story definitely takes place in your head. When you listen, it seems to happen in a little cloud all around it, like a fuzzy knit cap pulled down over your eyes"

— Robin Sloan, Mr. Penumbra's 24-Hour Bookstore

"*We will speak for the books.*"

...

"*Like the Lorax?*"

"*The Lorax speaks for the trees,*" *I remind her.*

"*Books are made out of paper. Paper is made out of trees.*"

"*What about e-books?*"

"*We can speak for them too.*"

"*Audiobooks?*"

"*Audiobooks speak for themselves.*" *She grins.* "*Get it?*"

— Paul Acampora, I Kill the Mockingbird

One of the biggest changes in the publishing industry right now involves audio books. While they have always enjoyed some popularity, especially with those professions who drive long distances, with digital distribution that popularity has surged. Adding to their popularity is the recent reduction in production cost, and the accessibility to various markets for audio that many writers now have.

What does this mean to indie authors, non-fiction, writers, and publishers of all kinds? It means that you need to consider audio books as a part of your wider distribution plan, if at all possible. But what does audio book production look like, and how can you make it work for you?

Select the Book You Want Read First

This is really important. The book you select should be one that has a following and has sold some copies anyway. The other good option is to do this with a new release. This gives you more formats and distribution options form the beginning. It is also a great way to revitalize your backlist. If you have books that have aged out and are no longer selling like they once were, an audio book can spark interest both in the new format and in the books you have already created.

The thing is you want the first book you start with to be one that the audio book will be successful and sell, and one that is easy to both record and distribute. It is also important to remember that audio books are priced by length, so while shorter books are easier to record and cost less to produce, you will also be selling them for less. It may take you longer to make your investment back, and shorter audio books may not sell the way longer ones do.

So, what is the criteria for choosing your first audio book? It's really up to you. Here are some general guidelines, but ones you can break:

- Choose a book that sells or has sold well or a new release.
- Choose something that is not too short, but also not too long. Your first audio book probably should not be a 400-page epic fantasy.
- Choose something that is easy to read and record. More on how to figure this out in a moment.

Now that you have made a choice of the what, it is time to decide who.

Choose a Narrator or Cast

Now that you have chosen a book, you need to choose who will read it, and the first question to ask and answer is whether you want a single narrator, a couple of narrators, or if you want to use an entire cast, like a movie only without the visual elements. The key to remember is this: the more people you have reading, the more it will cost (you have to pay them), and the larger your production costs will be (more editing is needed).

This is a discussion that literally hundreds of blog posts have been written about and you will find many about this aspect alone. The most important thing to keep in mind is that your writing is a business, and audio books are a part of that business. This means you need to make money when you are selling them.

Therefore, your first audio book should probably be one using a single narrator or maybe two, a male and a female. If you choose a professional narrator, you can find one that already has a following because people like the books they narrate and how they speak. This can have big marketing advantage for you.

Never narrate your own books, except possibly non-fiction titles. The reason? It feels very narcissistic, readers can tell it is you, and you often do not do as well reading your own stuff as you would someone else's. You are too close to it. Even if you have a great radio or theater voice, hire someone else.

If you have a cast, there is nothing wrong with you making an "audio cameo" as one of the minor characters, like authors and directors often do in their own movies. As with any rule, there are exceptions to this, but listeners often look at who narrated the book, and often won't purchase it if the author reads their own work.

And that is, after all, what creating the audio book is about. Selling books.

The Script

Your book is set up for reading, not for audio book production necessarily, and especially if you are working with a cast, you will need to create a script for the reader or readers. This is usually a pretty simple process, but if narrators are using different voices for each character then those need to be indicated, as simple things like pauses you would like added, etc.

You can often do this by simply having a program like Natural Reader or even Word or other writing programs read your work to you. Take notes as you go as to where you want pauses, voice changes, and other director's type notes then create a script from those notes.

Even if you are quick, this might take you a day or two. Allow time for that in your writing and production schedule to avoid frustration. Lastly, allow the narrator or a few members of the cast to look things over before you finalize the script to make sure it reads well. This will be key leading into the production process.

The Production Process

Once you have chosen a narrator or cast and finalized a script, you are ready to tackle the production process. This involves a few steps: recording, editing, and final production. What do those look like?

Recording is simply the narrator or cast reading your book. Most narrators narrate at around 9,000 words per hour, so if you have a 70,000-word book, that is just over 7 hours of reading. Narrators are usually paid by the word or by the group of words (for instance, $30 per 1,000 words). This means that your audio book will cost around $2,100 for just the audio recording, not counting the final production costs.

Editing is the process of taking that raw recording, stabilizing sound and eliminating mistakes: Editing essentially cleans up the recording. Ideally this should be done by a professional as well, since most authors do not have the experience to do this and do it well. There are of course exceptions, but most audio editors or sound engineers can do this really quickly: It should not cost you a great deal of money.

Final production is often done by the editor, and it simply consists of adding music, fades, sound effects if desired, and then producing a final audio file for you to upload to various distribution sites.

Distribution

Yes, overall audio books are another form of distribution, but they are also distributed several ways, and can be offered widely or on only a few services, such as Amazon Audible. However, wider distribution makes more sense with audio books just as it does with most eBooks.

This means you will want to not only offer your audio book on the big sites like Audible and Apple, but on smaller sites along with making it downloadable from your own site. The wider the distribution you have of your audiobook, the better, and the easier it will be to market to a broad, diverse market.

Marketing

We will cover this more in the next section of this book but suffice it to say that, like your eBooks and print books, audio books must be marketed to the right reader at the right time. More audio books mean listeners are more common, but it also means that there are more audio books out there, and yours needs to stand out. Discoverability is the biggest issue with audio the same as it is with other book formats.

We'll talk about this in detail soon, but the more formats your book is available in, the easier it will be to market all of the formats you have. This is the reason multiple formats are such a vital part of the distribution section of this book.

CHAPTER NINETEEN

WHAT'S NEXT?

"YOU SEE, bookshops are dreams built of wood and paper. They are time travel and escape and knowledge and power. They are, simply put, the best of places."

—Jen Campbell

"I always felt, if I can get to a library, I'll be OK."

—Maya Angelou

"What I say is, a town isn't a town without a bookstore. It may call itself a town, but unless it's got a bookstore, it knows it's not foolin' a soul."

—Neil Gaiman

We talked earlier about how print continues to be a good option for your books. The reason, other than marketing, is that there is a group of readers who prefer paper books to eBooks. There is also something grounding and real about holding a physical copy of your book in your hands, as we also talked about in the chapter on print books.

But there are two aspects of print distribution we did not touch on in great length in part because they deserve their own chapter and their own mention. Those are indie bookstores and libraries. Each is unique and serves their own purpose. If you, like me, grew up as a library kid, you know how much books could influence and shape the lives of young people.

In this chapter, we will approach Indie bookstores and libraries from the lens of all authors, but especially indie authors. The reason being is, like your writing business, these are businesses that are primarily interested in making a profit. This is especially true for indie bookstores as they operate on very small margins.

The Death of the Chain Bookstore

Much has been said about Amazon and the death of the chain bookstore, but for the moment we are going to ignore that debate. For the purpose of this book, we will touch briefly on their role with authors in that the death of the chain bookstore would have a huge impact on the publishing industry. The reason lies in both distribution and our next topic, marketing.

The reason we still need chain bookstores is that it continues to be the way more traditionally published authors distribute their work: that and simply for the sake of books. Because of the way Indie bookstores work and the margins they operate on, they cannot carry near the volume a chain can, nor are they able to keep them on the shelf for as long (more on that in a moment).

From a marketing standpoint, chain bookstores are the main driver that turns print books into bestseller books. Chain bookstores order in bulk from the publisher, often at a discount. In turn, the publisher is able to recognize a boatload of initial sales: these initial sales are to bookstores, not directly to readers, but that doesn't matter: Sales are sales; in the traditional publishing game, who the sale is to. With this model, bestselling books are not necessarily directly related to readership.

This is one of the reasons for the death of the chain bookstore. Chain bookstores pay more attention to publishers than readers, and the publishers, in kind, pay more attention to bookstore sales than reader sales. Books that don't sell end up on the discount table, and if they don't sell, are returned to the publisher and often "pulped" rather than put in boxes on a shelf in a warehouse. This means many of the books "purchased" are never actually sold to a reader.

This has less to do with Amazon and less-expensive books online and more to do with the fact that chain bookstores failed to adapt to the changing landscape and offer readers an experience. The largest chain remaining, Barnes and Noble, sells more than just books; they sell toys, coffee, records, and games nearly as much as they sell books. In some Barnes and Noble stores, they have tried to create an experience, but they still really heavily on publishers for input, marketing, and direction and will not deal directly with authors.

This is a huge source of frustration for Indie authors who reside in a given chain bookstore's area in that the store and their management, for the most part, ignore local Indie and self-published authors. Because of this underrepresentation, most regional authors struggle to sell their books in the chain bookstore, let alone schedule a signing or author event there.

With the takeover of Barnes and Noble by Waterstones, it is hoped that it will follow a similar pattern to the UK giant, and begin to adapt to a more local and Indie author friendly model. It's also likely that Barnes and Noble will start to focus further on reader experiences, events, and other things that bring in customers and drive readership.

Meanwhile, Amazon is opening physical bookstores, using the data they have about local buying habits to stock their shelves with books that will actually sell to readers. The stores are smaller than traditional chain stores. They much more customer focused, with kiosks where people can order books or eBooks, and displays of Amazon devices customers can put their hands on.

This works because the store offers an experience rather than just a place to buy books. They are a place to read, shop, and even relax for a bit.

Will chain stores fade away like dinosaurs? The question remains to be answered. Honestly, it would be bad for publishing and authors if they did, but unless they find a way to adapt, the end appears inevitable.

Indie Book Stores

Where does that leave us? It leaves us with the smaller, Indie bookstores. The Indie bookstore is a place where you can find local books, the classics, and some modern bestselling titles. These are places where you know the employees and owners; it is the place where events, readings, and book clubs happen.

For a while, it looked like many of these places were in real trouble. Some were. They, like their chain counterparts, did not adapt to the new publishing market and died untimely and sometimes ugly deaths. Those who survived understood they needed to give the reader an experience that was different than other bookstores. They needed to have a mix of local authors who actually sold books as well as the tried and true traditional books and classics that would appeal to a broad and diverse spectrum of readers.

What does this mean to indie authors though? It means that you must understand how these bookstores work. This is also true for the traditionally published author. The profit margin for the average Indie bookstore is very small. They can't afford to give shelf space to books that don't first meet certain standards, and second, sell well enough to justify the real estate. Here are some tips to having your book stocked at an Indie bookstore:

- If you self-publish, follow the production steps we outlined and maintain professional, good looking books that are well written and professionally edited.
- Approach the bookstore humbly. You are asking for something valuable from them, shelf space and exposure. Understand what that is, what it is worth, and treat them with respect.
- Give them a reason to invest in your book. It's not just about what they can do for you, but what you do for them. Treat this like you would a job interview and do a little research about the bookstore and the types of books they carry. How will you drive traffic to their bookstore, not just for your book but for other books as well?
- Understand the shelf life of your book. Even if you sell well, your books will probably be there for six months, maybe a little more, but once the "new" hype dies, unless you have a non-fiction book that is more evergreen and relevant over a long period of time, it just won't sell enough to justify them keeping it in stock. Exceptions to this general rule is if you release another book in a series, and that results in sales of both book one and two.
- Ultimately, if they say "no" to your book, feel free to ask

why: It is important to receive the rejection respectfully and with grace. You don't want to leave them with a bad taste around your brand. There are many valid reasons they may say "no" to your book which may include your book is one they don't feel they have a market for – possible they could point you to alternative places to sell your book: They could be full of local books at the moment and just not have room. Whatever the reason, use their "no" as an opportunity to build a positive relationship.

Just like writing, bookselling is a business. It is great for you to be front and center in the bookstore and get that discoverability and exposure, but your books need to sell to justify that. The bigger fan base you have locally, the more traffic you can drive to your local bookstore, the more likely they are to work with you.

The Library

I love libraries and love to see my books there. Just like bookstores though, libraries have limited shelf space and need to have books there that people actually check out. Your book needs to be attractive to readers. Libraries are a great place to get discovered, and many people go on to purchase books by authors they first found there. However, you should to be mindful of your approach.

First, make friends with your local librarian. It is a great place to do research and even write from time to time if you get tired of your home office. Besides that, there are readers there and libraries can be great places to have events, such as book launches and signings.

Libraries, also like bookstores, are changing and are taking on the role of community centers. They hold events, classes, and are about more than just books. That means if you need to be about more than just getting your books in the door and on their shelves.

Become an active participant in their programs and create extended relationships, and you may find you are more likely to have your books placed there. Likewise, your books are also more likely to be checked out by patrons who see and know you.

Seem like a lot of work and something you don't have time for? Then understand your library may not have time for you either. There are dozens of books written in your community by authors who are doing it like pros in addition to those who are in the self-publishing slush pile. Your library will engage with you as a pro if you engage with them like a pro.

There are also eBook programs at most libraries, and those programs may also be very beneficial to you. The technical key to taking advantage of your library is your professionally produced and distributed books need to have an ISBN in order to be available for libraries to purchase or carry as eBooks.

ISBNs are available a number of places and you should be familiar with your options. But keep in mind, if you have a free ISBN from Amazon or another source that is not tied to your name or your publisher's name, it will also be harder for you to get your book into the library.

If you operate like a pro, you will get noticed as a pro; distribution to bookstores and libraries will be easier for you, but it still takes a lot of hard work and tenacity. Ideally, you want to get noticed beyond your hometown but starting close to home and working your way out will get you there.

Serials, Podcasts, and Video

The future of the book has more than one path. There are extended opportunities through serials or series you could offer on your website to your fanbase via a subscription method. This works especially well for shorter novellas in a series. There are even emerging programs like Radish and Wattpad paid where you can offer these stories and make money from them.

Depending on your series and your topics, another great way to share your books and to promote them is through podcasting. More books and worlds are being shared this way all the time; the more authors who use it, the more popular it becomes.

While there are podcasts about writing, those are more for other writers rather than readers. That works if you have a book to sell like this one, where your audience is writers. However, that may not be the best place to promote your fiction work. Your readers only care so much about the writing and creation process. They care more about you, your characters, and what is coming next from you and other authors.

If you gain enough of a following, you actually make money on the podcast itself through sponsorships, advertising, and even affiliate marketing. in addition to its organic way of directing people to your work.

The kicker is that creating and producing a podcast is time consuming. You may want to appear on a podcast with other authors or even with readers initially. If you are able to split the work among a team, the process will be easier.

Books are also being shared through vlogs and other video platforms. It is easier than ever to transform your book into a short film or series: However, this also has become a crowded market. It can be time consuming, but by partnering with other creatives you could make it worth both your time and theirs.

What is the future of bookstores, books, and all of these other forms of sharing stories? The truth is, we don't know. At this point, you have committed yourself to writing as a business. Knowing what they are, how you might engage in them, and the best way to make money in that space will help to drive you towards future production and distribution mastery enabling you to achieve your goals in this business.

Next, we will look at some final thoughts on distribution before we move on to the toughest section, Marketing.

CHAPTER TWENTY

FINAL THOUGHTS ON DISTRIBUTION

"READERSHIP IS HIGHLY dependent upon format and distribution as much as it is on content."

— *Sara Sheridan*

"Making a product is just an activity, making a profit on a product is the achievement."

— *Amit Kalantri, Wealth of Words*

What can we conclude about all of the information shared about distribution thus far? There are a lot of opinions out there, and what works for one author might not work for another one. However, when it comes to being a successful writer and running your writing as a business, there are some common things we can conclude about distribution.

Wide Distribution is Best Use of your Time

Most other successful businesses do not rely on one source of income or one outlet for their product or service and nor should the professional writer. In fact, wide distribution is likely the wave of the future. The eBook may not be the ultimate format for reading in this digital age, but just as other, more searchable formats become available and editing tools become easier to use, the industry will once again change to remain viable and relevant to the demands of those who utilize it.

If you have all of your work vested in one place, or all your eggs in one basket - as the saying goes - you may have to make major shifts in your thinking in order for your distribution model to survive industry changes. There are those who say that exclusive Amazon distribution is not bad—you can always move your eggs if the basket is no longer working for you.

This is true, but the process to move all your eggs might cost you a lot of time and money, disrupting your writing business. Change is not easy for most and just as it would any other business, a business that has invested too heavily in one market or area of distribution will find what it takes to make necessary changes in their business model difficult, if it is deemed cost effective to do at all.

For most businesses, time is money and Writing as a Business is like most businesses: not many are able to ride the wave of change without a steady revenue stream: For those who do not build in a bit of flexibility into their long-term business goals, may find any change in the industry becomes very difficult and costly wave to ride out.

Print is not Dead

Print is still a great medium for distribution, especially for non-fiction books. Even for fiction, it gives you an outlet to readers you would not otherwise reach, and you never know when one of those readers will become one of your "superfans" and be a real evangelist for your work. Print books are expensive and sometimes the print book will come after your digital book has been out for a while and already earning you profits: This is especially the case for genre fiction.

Book signings, book tours and other events will still endear you to readers, and you can't really sign eBooks at a bookstore. Remember, indie bookstores and libraries are still a great place to be discovered and not having your books there only means that you are missing out on certain opportunities that could build your brand.

Audiobooks are Part of the Future

In the final section of this book we will be talking about marketing and having a number of formats to distribute makes your marketing easier. You will reach more and different types of readers. Audiobooks are a huge part of that and are experiencing a resurgence in digital media. They are cheaper and easier to make then they probably ever have been, so jumping into that market just makes sense.

The Future is Always Now

From subscription services to serials, from video to podcasting and other formats, the future is always here. It can be hard to determine what is best and what the next big trend will be. But it never hurts to try, as long as the monetary and time costs are reasonable. You may just find that group of readers or fans who will skyrocket your career.

Distribution Costs

With every type of distribution comes a new production cost and distribution cost. The idea is that those costs will not exceed the profits you make from any one avenue. If you find that costs are always exceeding your revenue, it could be that your marketing plan needs to be revised or it could also be that your costs are too high.

As with any other business, you need to routinely review what you are doing and be aware of your return on investment. Often with a writing business though, costs are not the issue: The issue, which is the biggest one for every single author no matter how successful and famous, is discoverability and marketing.

We'll tackle those next, with a focus on how to make your business a profitable one.

PART THREE

MARKETING

You must focus on using your time effectively every single day to get your message out."

— *Jim Edwards*

"...based on secondhand knowledge and first-hand experience, a successful online marketing cocktail looks like this: Equal parts hard work, talent and persistence, shaken for a long, long, long, long time, and some luck skewered onto a toothpick and thrown in for good measure."

--*Kristin Weber*

"Real marketing begins at the moment you conceive the central idea for the intended book and includes a clear sense of who the book is for, how it serves its audience, and how it fits with the competition."

— *David Cole*

Perhaps the most difficult section in this entire book to write about is marketing. The reason is simple. We are only able to talk about general principles in this book: The specifics change much too often to be of value. Realistically, we are not able to address specific marketing channels because those channels are ever changing and continuously evolving. While there are a few constants that have been successful methods for a long time, what works today may not work tomorrow.

The answer to the marketing is there are certain guiding principles a writer should follow to determine what to do and when to do it. The key is you must do something: you cannot just do nothing. A book that is not marketed will not sell. While a writer cannot control what will go viral or really catch on, the author can control their content.

You also need to understand the difference between marketing and advertising. In this section, we will include both under the broad umbrella of marketing, but the essential breakdown is this: Advertising costs you money and is usually about paying someone, a company, or an entity to promote your work for you in one way or another.

Marketing is word of mouth, work that you do to create awareness about your books: this includes social media and SEO. These things could cost you money, if you are paying someone to do them for you, but, if you do them yourself, they usually cost you time instead.

A book that is marketed and advertised well will sell provided that it is produced well and has been distributed to places where it can find an audience. Effective marketing efforts will cost you time, money, or both. In this section, we will focus on general marketing principles for authors, some timeless activities, and how to write a viable book marketing plan for each book you release.

CHAPTER TWENTY-ONE

THE BRIDGE BETWEEN DISTRIBUTION AND MARKETING

NO MATTER how strong your product, even if it easily fits into already established habits and anybody who tries it likes it immediately, you must still support it with a strong distribution plan."

--Peter Thiel

"Content is king, but distribution is queen and she wears the pants."

--Jonathan Perelman, Buzzfeed

There is a correlation you must understand when it comes to business: you can only market your products where you sell it. It would do you no good to try to market your book to Kobo readers if you do not distribute your book via Kobo. That seems obvious but stick with me for a moment while we explore this bridge between distribution and marketing.

Revisiting Exclusive vs. Wide Distribution

In the conclusion on distribution, we mentioned most of the time wide distribution is the answer. However, much like when we talk about search engines we talk about Google, most often when we talk about eBook distribution, we talk about Amazon. That is because at this moment, that is where most author revenue comes from. Concentrating on marketing a single point of distribution is frankly less expensive and complicated than promoting multiple channels. If you are not marketing your book in those channels, why offer it there at all?

This is where the debate really hits the ground. A book that is not marketed does not sell, but if your book is available and people have heard of it through other marketing channels, they might buy it where it is available. These are considered incidental sales: you must determine if those sales are worth the effort and the expense of marketing your book through these channels.

Another important aspect is Amazon offers built-in marketing tools exclusively for books that are available exclusively in Kindle format: These are rather powerful marketing options. If this has reopened the debate of wide or narrow distribution for you, good. This is a debate you may want to revisit often.

Print Marketing

The value you find true for Amazon exclusivity, you should also consider for print books. Libraries, bookstores, and other outlets can't carry your print book if you do not have them available. That means if you produce print books, marketing them should be a part of your overall strategy.

This doesn't mean ordering print copies and attempting to sell them yourself. This is known in some circles as the "back of my Buick" marketing method, but you can only cover so much territory on your own. You will require other marketing aids, such as ads and efforts through more traditional print distribution methods to place your books in bookstores and in libraries outside your immediate area.

If you choose to go the route of traditional publishing, your publisher may or may not necessarily market for you. Still, there is only so much they will do. Honestly, the best marketer for your book is you, the author, and your fans who spread the word to their circles for you.

This is a quick chapter, but intentionally so. Before we dive into the changing marketing channels and how to determine which ones will work, it is important to understand the bridge between all aspects of writing as a business. You must produce a good product for it to be marketable, and you must think about distribution channels when you are formulating your marketing plan.

This book is written in order: production, distribution, and marketing, but many steps happen simultaneously, not in a prescribed sequence. Some steps are revisited often for your older books along with the newer ones you are currently producing.

Next, we will tackle two of the primary, and perhaps the most important, pieces of any marketing plan.

CHAPTER TWENTY-TWO

YOUR BOOK BLURB

"MAYBE I AM WRONG, but I tend to the think of the back of book blurb as an advertisement. The only one we will get free forever!"

— *Dan LaBash*

Perhaps the most critical aspect of your marketing efforts is the marketing material you write about each book you authored. We often write these blurbs as an afterthought, but, in truth, they matter a lot.

Why? The first impression a reader has of your book is the cover. You need an eye-catching cover before you even think about your promotion options. Unless you are a cover designer yourself, your cover artist is one of the most crucial members of your production team.

The second is the book blurb: It should be strong and create reader interest. What does that mean? What elements should it include?

There is a simple formula, and it is important that you take your time editing this marketing material. You should also plan on revising it from time to time to freshen up your book and its rankings on Amazon. Let's take a quick look at them.

Compare Your Book to Others

This sounds simple, but there are a lot of books out there, and while yours is unique, you will find others you will be able to compare yours against. For instance, if you write romance or erotica, review the book blurbs for the top 100 selling books in that genre. What format do they use? How long are they? Imitate greatness so you do not have to reinvent the wheel.

The Fiction Formula

The fiction formula for a book blurb usually has three elements:

- The problem: What goes wrong in the book?
- A promised twist: Something will go wrong in the solution to the problem. Don't give that away to the reader, but hint that there will be one.
- The mood of the book: This can include hints to the setting, the type of story it will be, and maybe a story it compares to.

Why should you follow this formula? Simple. It has been proven to work over and over with thousands of books. It is not that you can't have your own take on it, but readers have certain expectations, and in some ways, it is your job to give it to them.

Start with a Hook

This is your only chance to make a first impression with your potential reader, so get them hooked by building interest right away. Remember, you want them to purchase and read your book, and this is the first step.

Your Blurb Should be Character Driven

The best stories are the ones that are driven by characters. When you present your problem and your promised twist, it should be in light of who your main character is and why the reader should care about them. It is much easier for a reader to relate to a person than a place or an event.

Insert a Cliffhanger

The first line is your hook: it is the one that entices the reader to read the blurb in the first place. The cliffhanger is another hook but with a potential twist that makes the reader want to open the book and read what you wrote inside.

For example: "Will he walk away, only to find that someone is willing to kill for his confession?"

This is character driven: the main character wants to walk away, but the twist is that he may not find it that easy. The stakes? His life, one of the highest risks you can give your hero.

Choose Your Words Wisely

There are certain words that speak to readers of certain genres. Love, affair, broken heart, and relationship are all keywords for romance readers. The same words would not work with a thriller or crime audience unless they somehow related to murder, clues, death, risk of life, and other keywords and phrases.

Be sure that the words and language you use relate to your genre and are consistent with your voice. If your readers think you are writing a thriller and find it to be a romance, they will be disappointed and leave you some negative reviews.

The tools you use to select keywords and categories, discussed in the next couple of chapters, are also the same tools you use to add keywords to your blurbs, something that can help with Amazon searches, Google searches, and search rankings on other book title sites.

Shorten it Up

Try not to fit too much in your blurbs. Keep them between 100-150 words, really a few simple sentences. A big block of text tends to deter readers from doing anything but skimming your blurb, and that could deter a sale.

Keep your sentences short. Short sentences make for faster reading. Keep paragraphs short too. Put white space between them so readers can see they are brief.

Test it Out

There are a ton of ways to test two different blurbs or opening lines, the ones you will usually use with ads on social media and Amazon, so use them. Don't guess which phrasing is best, ask your readers and fans, and test them on different platforms. Below is a list of how you may test your blurbs:

- Send sample blurbs to your email list via a survey.
- Post a couple of choices on social media and let your fans vote.
- Ask other writers or your writers' group for their opinion and feedback.
- Create a survey using Survey Monkey or other tools and gather other opinions from social media and a wider audience than just your email list.

The point is that this is your book, but your opinion is not the only one that matters when it comes to marketing materials. Get the opinion of both readers and professionals then refine and edit it until it is near perfect as possible.

This method is known as A/B testing, and you'll use it with ads, blurbs, covers and any other marketing and even writing things you can do.

Things You Can Add

After you have used up your 150 words, you can add some extra things that will sometimes get you more clicks or downloads. They are not essential, but any credibility you can gain with readers could help boost sales.

- Quotes by authors or reviewers: if you have quotes about your work and have permission to use, use them. This often will entice a reader to buy. The same is true of quotes from reviewers.
- Author awards: have you won awards for your writing? Share them at the bottom of your blurb. It shows readers that you are a professional, and they will pay more attention to your work.
- Number of Reviews: Do you have a lot of reviews on Amazon or other sites? Are they all five stars, or you have a very good review ranking? Share it here.

The key is for the reader to be intrigued by your work and to be assured that you have created a quality product for them to consume. This is the surest way to get them to push that buy button.

Common Mistakes

First, don't give away any spoilers. Usually there are a few summaries that you make of your book, and if you submit to a publisher or an agent, they may want the whole story in your summary. Your reader doesn't though. If they know the spoilers up front, they have no reason to read the book, and it won't be very satisfying if they do.

Second, avoid clichés and common stereotypes. Your book is unique, the blurb should be too. No one wants to read a story filled with clichés, and they won't want to read a blurb filled with them either.

Last, avoid comparing yourself to other authors, especially famous ones. This could result in disappointment in your readers, and it also projects a certain amount of ego on your part. If a reviewer has compared you to another famous author that is one thing, for you to do it yourself is a big negative.

The Non-Fiction Blurb

There are a couple of forms of non-fiction, and the book blurbs you should write that are dependent on the genre.

For instance, a memoir will more follow the fiction formula.

- The problem or conflict: What makes this part of your life story you are telling interesting?
- A promised twist: What is the surprise in your story that makes it worth reading? Remember, don't give anything away. Just hint at it.
- The mood of the book: Is yours a happy story, a sad story, one of triumph or defeat? What did you overcome to get where you are today?

The simple reason is this type of non-fiction is still a story and needs to follow that formula. For other non-fiction, like this book or others that offer instruction or advice, there is a slightly different formula:

- The problem: This is the problem your book will solve. In the case of this book, many writers do not understand the business they are in. This book helps explain it and offers strategies to navigating through it.
- The solution: How will this book help the readers solve the problem they have? Practical, step by step advice? Does it offer a plan for the reader to work through? How is it arranged?
- The mood of the book: Is this a get-tough, stick-with-it book fundamental to navigating an industry, or is it geared toward gentle correction and feel-good self-help? Is it made for anyone to read, or is it geared toward professionals who really know their stuff but want to venture deeper?

These things will let the reader know if your book is what they are looking for and may even determine how useful it is to them. Want good reviews and a good following for your non-fiction? Make the right promises in the book blurb and deliver on them between the covers.

The most important thing you will write is your book. It must be high quality, hook and hold the reader, and bring them to a satisfactory conclusion. However, the second most important thing is your marketing materials, which includes your book blurb. This is what will hook the reader and get them to buy and read the book in the first place. A poor blurb is sure to make your other marketing efforts for each book much more challenging.

Now that you have a good blurb, it is time to talk about SEO.

Before we talk about SEO for you, the author and your brand, we are going to talk about SEO on Amazon. SEO simply means Search Engine Optimization, and SEO relates to two things on Amazon: keywords and categories. These elements are essential to your book being discovered by the right readers at the right time.

CHAPTER TWENTY-THREE

AMAZON KEYWORDS

THE ULTIMATE SEARCH engine would basically understand everything in the world, and it would always give you the right thing. And we're a long, long ways from that.

--Larry Page

A world where everyone creates content gets confusing pretty quickly without a good search engine.

--Ethan Zuckerman

Why is Amazon search important? Simple. You want your book to be discovered among the literally hundreds that are being created each day. Amazon is the place where more readers go to find books than anywhere else in the world, so ranking well there makes a big difference for your revenue stream.

So, you have a good cover and a strong blurb. You now need to ensure your book is discoverable, and the way to do that is through keywords. Fortunately, Amazon gives you some great tools. You can choose up to seven keywords for your book, but it goes deeper than that.

Amazon allows key phrases, so one is able to add several keywords in one section. This means you may add combinations of word strings, such as "suspense thriller crime mystery" allowing your book to rank for each word yet using just one of the seven keyword slots you have been allotted.

Good news, right? Yes, it is, and that is just the start. However, for those slots to be effective you need to know what to fill them with. How do you figure that out?

Amazon Search

One way you can do this is through Amazon search. As you start to search anything on Amazon, there is an autofill option that fills in the rest of the phrase for you. The phrases that come up when you start typing are things other users have already searched for.

Like Google, Amazon wants to give users the best results for whatever they are searching for. Also, like Google, Amazon does not tell users the secrets of their algorithms and how they figure out which searches come up first. We'll talk about that more in the next chapter, when we talk about SEO for your brand as an author.

To determine this on your own, you can go on Amazon and type these phrases in yourself. The only problem? These terms are influenced by what you have searched for before. If you sign out of your Amazon account and search that way, you will get a better idea. This can be rather time consuming, but all that research could be worthwhile.

There are tools that will help you do these searches and save you a lot of time.

Publisher Rocket

One of the most touted of these services is Publisher Rocket. This is a tool that helps you search for those keywords and phrases that best fit your book and genre. It is not a cheap tool, but for most authors, it is well worth the expense, especially if they are writing and publishing books fairly often.

To its credit, Publisher Rocket has a lot of other marketing tools you could use market your book more efficiently and effectively. From my experience, the keyword tool is perhaps the most powerful. It provides you with phrases readers are actually searching for on Amazon every day.

These phrases change, of course, over time. So, you can use Publisher Rocket to do your research again and change your keyword phrases accordingly. In fact, you should at least evaluate your backlist keywords every time you release a new title. If you are going to invest in one tool for your marketing, Publisher Rocket is one that you should seriously consider utilizing.

Restrictions

Of course, Amazon is not the wild west, and there are rules. You cannot use keywords such as other authors' names, ones that might falsely associate your books with them. You also cannot include things that relate to sales, like the words "bestselling" or "top seller."

For the sake of integrity, there are also keywords you should not include. You should not include words that do not relate to your title. It might be confusing for general users who come across your book in an inappropriate search.

Think of it this way: if one of your characters is named Christian in your erotica book, do not include this word in your keywords. Someone looking for Christian fiction might come across your book in a search, leave a damaging review or report it to Amazon; these are questionable associations that could be potentially devastating to your sales.

Most of this is pretty much common sense, but the main takeaway is that you do not have to guess what words people are looking for when they search for your books; with the help of these tools, you will ensure that you appear in those searches. In business, this is called making a data driven decision.

Of course, to rank in those searches you will to have to sell enough books to outrank other books in that search term. KDP Rocket will also tell you how competitive some searches are, and how hard it will be to rank for them. This gives you a clue to which keywords and phrases to choose from.

Either way, do your research. See what other books are ranking for your keywords and make adjustments accordingly.

Next, we will talk about how to increase your book rankings and, in turn, your book sales by using a couple of different types of marketing channels. We will start with those that are free.

CHAPTER TWENTY-FOUR

FREE ADVERTISING CHANNELS

"NOTHING OF VALUE IS FREE. Even the breath of life is purchased at birth only through gasping effort and pain."

— Robert Heinlein

"It's unwise to pay too much, but it's worse to pay too little. When you pay too much, you lose a little money - that's all. When you pay too little, you sometimes lose everything, because the thing you bought was incapable of doing the thing it was bought to do. The common law of business balance prohibits paying a little and getting a lot - it can't be done. If you deal with the lowest bidder, it is well to add something for the risk you run, and if you do that you will have enough to pay for something better."

— John Ruskin

There is much talk about free marketing channels, and if I had a dime for every time I heard an author say, "I can't afford to pay for ads" I would be able to afford a lot more ads myself. There are two important aspects to understand about marketing and ads when it comes to the word "free."

Everything Has a Cost

If you have not learned this lesson already and did not get that impression from the quotes above, let me emphasize it to you again. There is no such thing as a free lunch, and there are also no such thing as "free" ads for your books that have proven themselves effective.

First, understand the most valuable thing you have as a writer is your time. You only have a limited amount of it, and how you spend it will determine how successful you are. Even websites that let you list your book on them for free will cost you in time and the effort it will take to post your books in their directory.

How effective are these free directories? Not very. It used to be that getting your book listed in these directories could be good for your book's Google ranking, however many directories no longer have good web authority and click throughs to your book from them will be rare. You are better off improving your SEO for your book instead.

Second, often those directories are also selling some kind of promotional services. They want you to use their services to promote your page on their directory. This then turns into a paid ad, but an ad that drives traffic to their website not yours. Your efforts, time, and resources are better served purchasing a link for your book on Amazon or through another distribution channel.

How do these sites make money? Many of them use affiliate links, so that is how they earn money by promoting your book. Affiliate links, if you don't know, give a percentage of the sales that happen to the referring site. You can even use affiliate links on your own site to help you make even more money from your own sales and even books and other items you review on your site. While that is another discussion for another time, I can help your writing business make a little extra money.

This means the more books you sell, the more they make. That is often what makes these sites looking into and at least listing your books on. Again, you do have to weigh the time and effort it will take you to do so.

Remember if it sounds too good to be true, it probably is. Often after you follow all the steps to have your book listed, there will be a paid option that promises to be truly effective. More on figuring out whether a particular channel is worth the price or not will be discussed in a later chapter.

Social Media Works, Right?

Let's debunk a few myths right here. First of all, social media is not free, at least effective social media, because it costs you time. Secondly, you need to determine if your followers on social media are really your target audience.

The most common author mistake on social media is to friend primarily other authors. I mean, we all want to have friends with shared interests, right? Correct, but other authors are not the ones who will buy your books unless your book is for authors, like this one.

Secondly, social media is for just that: being social. It is not the place to sell books, or at least not the appropriate place to be salesy. Your friends will quickly tune you out and ignore you when all you post are "buy my books" links. They will quickly understand that you have no interest in them but are merely there to push something. Trust me, if it does not work for Nike, Red Bull, or Dean Koontz, it won't work for you.

Third, Facebook and other social media sites make personal posts, photos, and video more prominent in your friends feeds for one very important reason: they survive on ad revenue, so they are not going to promote your book links, your blog posts, and other similar items for free. This type of content is for your business page, and you must pay to promote posts if you want more people to see them.

Facebook groups where you can promote your book are often full of other authors trying to do the same and are not very effective at all. If you are in a group of actual readers, you can't just promote your own work. You will need to engage in discussions and be an active, social part of the group. If the group interests you and you get some personal satisfaction from it, your time may not be wasted, but if you are just there to sell books, you might find yourself putting out a lot more effort than the return you get.

This, again, reinforces that social media is not free, at least not for business. Your writing is a business, so you will have to pay for ads to make social networks effective. To make those ads matter, you need to have the right target audience following your page and beyond. We'll talk more about these ads in a moment.

Exchanges of Work

There is the thought of using your writer network and that of other writers to spread things to their readers about you and to your readers about them. There is actually some validity to this, but there are also some dangers. Here are a few principles to keep in mind.

- **Guest Post Exchanges:** These are actually a great idea, and they are almost free. They do take work to write a post about your book or story, and it also takes your time to post the other person's post on your site. If they have enough of a following, this could make your efforts truly worthwhile.

- **Review Exchanges:** The problem with review exchanges is that it is hard to get honest reviews, and Amazon has cracked down on the deceptive nature of this type of trade. This does not mean you cannot review other author's work, and they cannot review yours, it means you must be careful not to do those things exclusively. It can get both of your reviews removed from Amazon, including any of the other reviews you have left on books or products.

- **Promotional Exchanges:** These are usually done on social media, and while they can be good, be aware of the other person's network. If yours is full of other authors, theirs might be as well. Writing the posts and posting theirs does cost you time, and if the return is not worthwhile, your efforts are probably best spent elsewhere.

- **Bookfunnel and Similar Services:** There are groups in place for promotional exchanges, although you will need to pay to use these services. However, they are often worth the money, as you get access to other writers and their network of readers. These authors are often vetted for you, and you can choose those promotions that actually relate to your book and your genre.

The most important thing to understand is that work exchanges are still work. You will find that the time you spend marketing is limited, or it should be, and you will need to make the most of it. Free options, while at first, they seem desirable, are not always the most efficient use of that time.

We'll talk a bit more on a few of these methods along with paid methods in the next couple of chapters.

CHAPTER TWENTY-FIVE

(ALMOST) TIMELESS PAID MARKETING METHODS

"MARKET like the year you are in!"

--Gary Vaynerchuck

"Marketing is no longer about the stuff that you make, but about the stories you tell."

--Seth Godin

"If you have more money than brains you should focus on outbound marketing. If you have more brains than money, you should focus on inbound marketing."

--Guy Kawasaki

Book marketing is changing. There are few strategies that work all the time, but this doesn't stop companies from popping up who will promise hundreds of sales if you let them blast out your book to the world through their social media channels, email lists, or some other mystical and magical medium.

The truth is, most of these don't work in the way you would like, and by using many of them you won't even break even on the cost of the promotion. More on how to tell if those work or not in the next chapter. For now, though, let's look at some nearly timeless paid marketing methods that do work, why they work, and what you can expect to get for your investment.

Before we do, let's clarify for a moment. Paid marketing is really advertising, which means paying someone to market your work. This is a critical difference to remember when talking with marketing companies or hiring a pro to do some marketing and promotions work for you.

Guest Posting/Guest Blogging Tours

There is, among authors, a debate about how well these still work, and whether or not readers still read blogs to find their next book to read. However, there are still some benefits of guest posting and guest blog tours.

For a moment, we will talk about guest posting, because sometimes you can do this for free. All it will cost you is your time to write the post, and the blog owner will post your blog to encourage more traffic to their website. They are, of course, counting on you to share this blog with your network, which you should.

What kind of return do you get from guest posting? Well, there are a couple clear benefits, but they overlap with the benefits you receive from a blog tour, so let's look at those first.

A blog tour is similar to a guest post, only someone else organizes for it you to guest post on several blogs over a set period of time.

Typically, you are expected to pay for organization costs of the tour. Often these bloggers are also reviewers, so you could garner a number of book reviews at the same time.

Understand what you are paying the person to do is organize the blog tour through their network of bloggers or the placement of the blog post themselves. You are not paying for reviews. This is a good deal, because instead of using a lot of time to reach out to bloggers to see if you can borrow their blog for a day, instead you are only spending time writing posts and answering occasional interview questions.

What do you get from this? The benefits of guest posting and blogging are actually pretty substantial even though you might not get an immediate spike in sales.

- **Backlinks:** In a few chapters, we will talk about link building to your website to increase your Google ranking. A guest post or better yet, a blog tour is one of the best ways to build links to your site, even though they might not be the highest authority links out there.
- **A New Audience:** The blogger clearly has an audience of their own, and they are introducing you to their friends. This gives you a bigger venue for your work.
- **Sales:** While you might not see a huge spike in sales, if you write for several blogs in a row on a tour, you will see some.
- **Reviews:** Most of our author income comes from Amazon, and reviews are key to your Amazon rankings and sales. Through blog tours, you will often gain reviews from the bloggers and others who follow their blog.

The problem with guest blogging and blog tours is that the gains you see are often slow and over an extended period of time. While you won't earn back your money or see that ROI or return on investment right away, the ranking increases you see in both Google and Amazon may make them well worth your time and effort.

The Golden Channels

There are some book promotion channels, such as Bookbub, are considered the Holy Grail of book promotion outlets. Bookbub offers two ways to get onto their mailing list and reach their extensive audience.

The first is that you may apply to have your book featured in their email blast, which is huge. This is very expensive, but it can yield great results. The cost depends on your genre, but you can't just pay and get your book featured. There is an application process and only a few books are accepted at a time. Many authors try a dozen times or more before getting in, and many never make it in at all.

The other method is to purchase Bookbub ads. These are actually fairly affordable as ads go. While they don't get the reach the email blasts do, Bookbub has one thing going for it: they have an amazing following of readers who get their newsletter and visit their site looking for books.

You will need a certain number of good reviews to get into the better channels, or your book will have to be brand new, yet still recommended. This is why getting reviews quickly matters. It not only increases your Amazon ranking, but it also provides you more marketing opportunities that you could leverage.

There are other great promotional tools that work consistently well: Kindle Nation Daily combined with Book Gorilla and ereader News Today to list a couple. As mentioned above, we'll outline how to vet these channels in the next chapter, but for now understand that there are some paid channels that work well, and there are new ones gaining traction all the time.

Amazon Ads

You have probably seen these ads while you browse on Amazon, and the likelihood is that you have clicked on one or more of them. The reason? Amazon is really good at targeting you with relevant books leveraged from your past purchases.

Before Amazon really starts to recommend a book on its own, an author needs around 50 reviews and some pretty stellar sales numbers. However, you can, through Amazon marketing, pay for targeted ads. There are a couple of ways to do so:

- You can target your books those who visit the pages of certain authors. If you choose the right authors that your books are most like, you may get a lot of sales.
- You can target a genre or search term. When a user searches for your type of book, you come up in the search results as a sponsored ad.

Which of these is best? The answer is that it depends, and you should probably test both using a marketing method called A/B testing. This tells you where to put the money on your next ads. We will cover that method briefly in a later chapter.

There are a number of ways to control your Amazon ads, including setting spend limits, targets, and more. This enables you to hopefully reach your ideal reader at the ideal time. Through testing, these ads can be truly effective.

Other Targeted Ads

Just like any other marketer, the better targeted your ads are, the more effective the ad. In other words, if you are a non-fiction author who has written a guide to bowling, taking out an ad for your book in a bowling magazine or on a bowling website is a great idea. You are reaching your ideal reader where they already are.

For some books, Google pay-per-click (PPC) ads work well if your topic is relevant enough and people search for it in Google. The point here is that targeting your ideal reader where they are surfing the web anyway and is one of the best ways to see a return on your investment.

Hiring a Pro

Does all this sound a little daunting? It is, and it takes a tremendous amount of time and effort. But when will you be ready to hire a pro to do all this for you? That depends on you. If you have limited time and don't want to research and learn all this stuff on your own, hiring a pro from the start can make a huge difference to your sales. Besides, they have done a lot of testing with a lot of authors and others in your genre. This can save you a lot of expense and time in the long run.

The thing is, you will need to keep writing, otherwise you won't make the money back you spend on that pro just on one book. However, several books being marketed at the same time can result in substantial income. Your writing business, the business of your book, often requires an investment, and you won't always see that money back right away.

It is important to point out that vetting the pro you hire is essential. Ask for references and review their track record. See if the authors they are helping are actually selling more books. Do not be afraid to ask lots of questions. Just like vetting ad channels, which we will talk about next, you should do your due diligence and research to determine which marketing pros are just after your money, and which ones will actually deliver on what they promise. There are hundreds of author forums out there: Google the person or company's name and see what others are saying about them.

There are only a few book marketing techniques that are truly timeless. Even those may fade over time. The point is that you must invest in advertising and marketing, and you must stay on top of what is working or hire a pro to stay on top of it for you.

Also understand this: even if you are traditionally published, most of the time a publisher will not do the marketing work and pay for advertising for you. Want to earn back that advance and actually make some money in the process? You may have to pay for these types of ads yourself.

Going any deeper on this topic in this chapter would be a futile exercise. Book marketing and advertising is in constant flux. Just stick with it. Don't quit, and you'll find the right channels where it really pays to invest your money.

CHAPTER TWENTY-SIX

VETTING MARKETING CHANNELS

"EVERYTHING WE HEAR IS AN OPINION, not fact. Every-thing we see is a perspective, not truth."

– Marcus Aurelius

The customer expects you to have knowledge of their stuff, not just your stuff."

– Jeffrey Gitomer

Let's be clear about one thing: Writing is a business. On the flip side, the business of helping writers write better and sell their work is another business all its own. While you are hiring a marketing firm or paying an advertising channel to help you sell your books, they will, at the same time, try to market their services to you.

In order for you to push buy or to book a promotion with their site, you need to believe that it is going to work. But should you take their word for it? Of course not. You would not hire an editor based on them telling you they are a good editor, or you shouldn't. You would look for word of mouth, references, and ask to see other things they might have edited.

The same thing is true for marketers, but where do you find that word of mouth, and how to you verify that their service is working. How do you know if your ad copy was bad, or their service just does not work? The truth is, there are several methods for vetting marketing channels and making sure they will work for you. Here are some quick and easy tips.

Word of Mouth

Remember that word of mouth is largely a two-way street. People share with you their experiences, and as you try different marketing channels, you should share yours as well. However, most of the time if you are about to try a marketing channel, someone else has tried it and reported their results. Taken with several other reviews, you will develop a good picture of what return you could expect on your investment.

When looking online, here are some things to keep in mind, as nearly anyone can review something, and they may have alternative reasons for posting a negative review.

- Note who posted the review and check out their books on Amazon. How long have they been out? How many reviews do they have, and how do they rank? Are the covers professionally designed? These are all things readers look at too and can affect sales results.
- How long ago was the review posted? Services try to get better year over year, just as you try to become a better writer. A review posted two years ago may not reflect how good the service is currently.

- How many similar reviews are there? Different books, different genres, all sell differently and work differently with marketing channels. Look for genres similar to yours, books similar to yours, and judge the channel accordingly.

So, where do you find these online reviews? There are a number of places, and you should look in all of them if possible, especially if you are planning to invest a lot of money in a particular venue. If you have several books, you might want to use them multiple times. Here are some quick places to look.

- **Google:** Simply Google the name of the promotion or advertising company followed by the word "reviews." Usually, many examples will pop up right away unless the service is brand new.
- **K-Boards:** A lot of writers are on K-Boards and talk about a lot of stuff - from writing craft to business. You will typically find a discussion about the marketing channel you are thinking about using with several contributors.
- **Facebook:** There are a lot of author groups on Facebook, some useful, some not. The useful ones will have discussions about books and the business of publishing. The rest will be filled with authors trying to sell their books, mostly to other authors. Vet groups carefully, through word of mouth and what you see in the groups, but there is probably a group of professionals dedicated to your genre. Often you will have to apply to join, and there will be clear rules about discussions and marketing your own books and services.

- **LinkedIn:** Mostly for professionals, LinkedIn has some good, professional author groups. There are also some that are similar to Facebook, but not as many. There tend to more rules, you often have to be accepted into a group, and there are rules you must follow to continue to participate.
- **Quora, Reddit, and More:** There are many places online that offer groups, and some are more useful than others. Find your place, where you are comfortable, and live there.

While online groups are wonderful, sometimes there is nothing that beats sitting down with a group of professionals and talking business. Ideas come out with discussion that might not have been brought up otherwise. Legitimate feedback is offered, and besides, you just meet some really cool people.

Writer's Groups

You should be in authors' groups, both online and in person if possible. This does not mean you have to devote hours to them, because you need to keep your focus and be productive. However, these groups should be a constant source of support for you, and an avenue for you to be supportive of other authors.

The drawback is that in-person groups have the potential to be a real waste of time. If you are looking for professional interaction, it can be truly frustrating. Nearly anyone will call themselves a writer or an author, but that does not mean they have anything to contribute or that they will take advice either. The community of professional writers is usually pretty tight and difficult to find and break into.

Why is this? Because we have blurred the definition of what a professional writer is, and what that means in reality. With the advent of self-publishing, even the term "published author" does not mean the same thing to one person as it might to another. Therefore, professionals (including me) are reluctant to join groups.

Here are some things to clarify and consider when looking for a group of authors to work with and seek advice from. Remember, at this point you are not looking for a critique group. They have their place, but that is back in the production stage. At this point, you are looking for a professional group, like a mastermind group. You want to talk business, from self-publishing to traditional, marketing but on a deep level, and not waste time on trivia or beginner type discussions.

For instance, as we examined before, you can get some marketing for free, but for great marketing, you will have to pay. That discussion should not even be on the table in a Mastermind group. Everyone should know about A/B testing and what that means. When vetting group members, here are some things that matter most.

- How many collective titles have those in the group published? If the answer is one or two, unless those titles were immediate best sellers or sell well regularly, you might be in the wrong group.
- How are they published? Is there a mix of some self-published, some hybrid, and other traditionally published authors? This gives you the widest perspective on what is really happening in publishing. All of these things have their place.
- What are the goals of the group? What is everyone trying to accomplish? Do those goals line up with yours?

Probably one of the most important things about a group is that you relate to the people in it and are able to align with their goals. You should also look for a group where you have something to add, where there are writers more experienced than you, and some who are less experienced. Vetting marketing channels will require a variety of people to give you accurate word of mouth information.

Site Guarantees

So far, we have talked in this chapter just about word of mouth both online and in person. There are other ways to vet marketing channels to ensure they work. One of these is the promises that the site itself offers you. Many, like Book Butterfly, will guarantee that your book will earn out your investment or they will offer you another listing for free.

It is in the best interest of the sites that your book sales succeed. As we covered earlier, even free sites make money from affiliate links, but only if you sell books. By listing only high-quality books, sites often have great advice about your book listing and will offer a guaranteed number of sales.

This is really difficult for them to do, but worthwhile because of two things: first, you and other authors have a protected investment, and are assured that you are not wasting your money. In return, the site gets better word of mouth and more customers like you who list their books on the site and in their newsletter. In turn, this practice expands the number of readers who return for recommendations, making their business more successful.

One sure way to vet a marketing channel is simply to get a guarantee, and if the site does not meet their limits, look at how close they came and why your book might have "missed' with their readers list. This can do a lot to inform your future promotions and where you should spend your money going forward.

Simple Analytics

Here is another simple way to determine what works. If there is little information or only a few reviews online about a marketing channel, try them and do some simple analytics. How does this work?

Well, if you are self-published, you can watch the number of sales on your KDP dashboard and in other sales channels, usually updated every couple of hours. Watch this instead of your Amazon rankings, since Amazon rankings can be deceiving. The number of books you sell in the time of the promotion, times the amount you earn from each book (especially if you had to put them on sale) will tell you how much you made vs. how much the promotion cost.

To be really sure what effect a promo is having, isolate it. This can be problematic, because the best way to really affect sales is to run more than one promotion at one time. While some promo sites offer you a link where you can watch your sales for that day through their site and determine ROI that way, not every site does so, especially if the site is new.

However, if you are trying something new, stopping other promos and isolating one for a day or two can help determine ROI. The key is to understand that you might have residual sales coming from other promotions, so do your best to use unique links for each promo with bit.ly or another similar service, and track sales vs. cost.

When you are new, if you don't break even on a promo, but you come close, it was probably worth it anyway. You got your book in the hands of a new audience and that is always worth something.

This goes back to setting goals and expectations from the start. Understand that some promos are as much about spreading your name and exposure as they are about direct sales. The sales will come over time, when you run more promotions all the while your name and your book becomes more familiar to readers.

The Ugly Truth

The sad part of marketing for authors is that there are rip-off sites out there. Some provide you with false or misleading sales numbers and data. Others have relatively small lists of readers, and so it is hard for you to recoup your money or the time you spent setting up a promo package.

The truth of the matter is that more people make money off promises to help writers than those who are actually writers. Some prey on new or naïve writers, which, if you are reading this book, you are not any longer. Many sites make unrealistic promises no one can guarantee so be wary of sites that look too good to be true.

If you work in this industry long enough, you will probably get suckered in to at least one scam and get burned. Learn from it and move on, understanding this is one of the costs of doing business. You are chasing a dream, and someone is going to try to sell you things to help you accomplish that dream. Some offers will pay off, and others will not. Don't take it personally or get down on yourself. Keep your confidence and move on, always marketing.

I'm not saying this is not hard to do. It is hard to lose time and money and not let it affect your self-esteem. As with any business, writing is less about what has passed and more about what is next. Keep moving forward no matter what and look for new opportunities. The more you apply these vetting principles, the more successful your marketing efforts will be.

CHAPTER TWENTY-SEVEN

THE IMPORTANCE OF REVIEWS

"THE CRITIC'S aim should be to interpret the work they are writing about and help readers appreciate it, by defining and analyzing those qualities that make it precious and by indicating the angle of visions from which its beauties are visible. But many critics do not realize their function. They aim not to appreciate, but to judge; they seek first to draw lines about literature and then bully readers into accepting these laws."

— David Cecil

"A writer hopes never to offend, but if he must, pray let him offend the gods before the reviewers."

— *Chila Woychik,* On Being a Rat and Other Observations

"It's the Yelp effect. Every halfwit who eats food suddenly thinks he's a food critic. And don't get me started on people "reviewing" books they didn't even read. Who needs information, when you can have an uninformed opinion?"

— Oliver Markus Malloy, Why Creeps Don't Know They're Creeps - What Game of Thrones can teach us about relationships and Hollywood scandals

Reviews. They are the bane of every writer's existence. Too many great reviews, and you may feel like your book has finally arrived. Even if you have a whole bunch of good reviews, one bad one can seemingly ruin your day. However, book reviews are more important to marketing than they are to your ego, and that means you have to send your books to reviewers.

But let's look at some facts really quickly. Why are reviews so important? Here are several reasons.

Reviews Matter to Future Readers

Reviews of your books tell readers what the book is about and what other readers found to be enjoyable about it. It makes a huge difference in whether a person will buy your book or even read the free selection you have on Amazon. This is also why it is important to have a variety of reviews from more people than just your family and friends. In fact, reviews from professional or high-ranking reviewers, even if they are 3- or 4-star reviews instead of 5 stars help readers trust your book more.

Even bad reviewers don't necessarily hurt your book's chances to resonate with a reader. Sometimes the reviewer will point out something that potentially offended them that will resonate with another reader. Don't be discouraged. The best thing for your book is to have as many reviews as possible, and a variety of ratings that leans toward the good end of the spectrum. Obviously, if you are getting a lot of bad reviews, that can really hurt your sales.

Know that not everyone will like your book. However, the more a reader knows about it before they start, the more likely they are to leave it a good review when they are done reading.

Reviews Matter to Amazon

You need to have a certain number of reviews for Amazon to start promoting your book in a big way. If you have 50 or more, they will feature it in their email blasts. If you have 100 or more, other promotions of your work will happen without you triggering them.

Reviews also affect your Amazon rankings. The more reviews your book has, the higher your rank in their algorithm, which means more people are being exposed to your book page. This usually translates to more sales. Remember, a big part of marketing is about discoverability, one of the hardest things for authors to achieve without some marketing help. Reviews help you get that exposure and be discovered.

The other part about reviews is they let Amazon know you are legitimate as an author. There are literally hundreds of authors who self-publish and rarely sell any books at all: The likely future those books is they will start disappearing from the Amazon listings. The more reviews you have, the less likely it will affect your backlist. Of course, you should continue to market those older book releases anyway.

Reviews make a huge difference on Amazon, but on other sites as well. Securing reviews should be a high priority marketing strategy.

Paying for Reviews

Amazon wants one thing when it comes to reviews. They want honest, unbiased reviews that are from actual readers, not just your friends and family. That means you have to ask your readers, those who have purchased your books, to leave reviews for you. While you will not know every reader, there are ways to contact them and ask for reviews; we will cover those in a moment.

You will also see plenty of offers from people to leave reviews for your book, many of them for money. There is one issue with this: it is strictly against Amazon policies and can land you in big trouble as an author if you get caught. Does that mean you should never pay for reviews or that all of them will get you in trouble? Not exactly. There are other ways around it.

Blog Review Tours: We talked previously about blog tours that are geared to get bloggers to read and review your books. These usually cost money and are sometimes through an agency, but you are not paying for reviews, at least not strictly speaking.

What you are paying for is for the agency to organize the tour, for the advertising you get from the posts on the blog, and for the time of the blogger to link to your book and your website from their own. Technically, this is not paying for reviews and is a generally accepted practice. Sometimes reviewers who have abused the Amazon system can no longer post there, but they may still post reviews on other outlets.

Professional Reviewers: There are some professional review sites that charge for reviews, and that Amazon will accept. These change from time to time, but Kirkus reviews, Publisher's Weekly, and other similar sites are among them. Are these reviews worth your money? That's a good question.

The review you get on their site and the resulting advertising are sometimes helpful, but the review itself may not be. It depends on your book and how many other reviews you have. If you have a whole bunch of legitimate reader reviews, this should be seen more as an advertising expense rather than as paying for reviews.

They do get you quotes you can use in those marketing efforts, reviews that are backed by a recognizable name. That name alone may convince some readers to pick up your work.

Other Reviewers: You can pay for reviews and hope you do not get caught. The review system is broken in many ways, but unfortunately it is the only one we have at the moment. Other authors in your genre might be paying for reviews, and that might give them an advantage over you for a short period of time. Is it worth the risk? For most authors, probably not unless that reviewer has a huge following.

Sources for Reviews

So, if you don't want to pay for reviews, how do you find reviewers? Here are some simple tips that work well for most authors.

- **Have a Street Team:** Offer for your readers to join a street team where they get access to books early and even free of charge as long as they leave a review. This can help you by ensuring you have a lot of reviews right after your book release. Offer other freebies and contests for your street team from time to time as well to keep them engaged.
- **Appeal to Your Readers:** Have an email subscription list and send out a request to them to review your work, especially if they have purchased it directly from where they will leave the review. This makes a big difference as well.
- **Send Out Appeals on Social Media:** Get in touch with your social media followers and ask them for reviews. Most understand their importance and will help you if they can. Not everyone can write a great review,

but often you can at least get a star rating and a few words of encouragement from them.

- **Contact Amazon Reviewers Directly:** There are lists of Amazon reviewers and you can see who have reviewed similar books to yours. Email them and ask them if they would like to review your work. Include a detailed pitch, and ask them what format they would like the book in. Not all of these will respond, but many will, and you can build a list of reviewers to send every book you publish to.

- **Net Galley:** One source for great and professional reviews is Net Galley. The cost for having your books on Net Galley is prohibitive for most Indie publishers. However, there are cooperatives and some public relations companies that can enable you to get your books in front of these reviewers. Many are librarians and book sellers, so it can also help increase your sales.

The idea is to outreach as much as possible. Market your work directly to reviewers, and you will greatly help boost your other marketing efforts.

Reviews Matter to Promotion Sites

Some of the best paid promotion sites ask that your book have a certain number of good reviews before they will promote it unless it is a recent release. This means that to get on Bookbub, Ereader News Today, and other really effective advertising sites, you need between 10-20 reviews, and for Bookbub, more is better.

And again, reviews matter to their readers. When they click on the link to your book, the more reviews you have, the more likely they are to buy your book.

Think of your own buying habits. If you see a product or a book for sale, typically you read about the product to see if it has the features you want and need, but you also read the reviews and see what others think before you press buy. A whole bunch of one-star reviews with issues tells you a lot about whether you want to purchase that product or not.

Other Advice on Reviews

As an author, celebrate good reviews and try to learn from bad ones. Sometimes the things pointed out have nothing to do with your writing or you as an author but have everything to do with the reader and their preferences. Sometimes they are things you can change and improve in your later work.

As a rule, though, don't comment on reviews, either good or bad. It just makes you look insecure: Besides, you have better things to do with your time anyway. Just keep writing. Of course, if a reviewer contacts you directly on social media or through your website, respond and thank them for their review and feedback. Just don't do it on Amazon, iBooks, Goodreads, or similar places.

The other advice, and advice it is much harder to follow, is to ignore bad reviews as much as possible. Don't take them personally. Your writing won't be for everyone, and even the best writers have made mistakes or had books that were not as good as others. Let them go and use whatever tools you need to do so.

Also, as a rule, almost never contest reviews unless they are malicious. It is a waste of your time and could actually discourage others from reviewing your work in the future. If your ex is 1-star bombing your books, there is little to nothing you can do about it that won't seem just as petty and malicious as their actions. It's best just to let it go.

Reviews are a key part of your marketing success, and the more legitimate ones you receive, the better. Use every technique you can but be sure you are not cheating the Amazon algorithm. Play by the rules, but never underestimate the importance of each and every review when it comes to marketing and your overall promotion strategy.

CHAPTER TWENTY-EIGHT

YOUR GOOGLE RANKING

"GOOGLE ONLY LOVES you when everyone else loves you first."

--Wendy Piersall

"The best place to hide a body is the second page of a Google search."

--Anonymous

As a writer, you need to have your own website and blog, you need to post regularly, and you need to deliberately link to it to other reputable sites.

Why? Because when people search for certain keywords or phrases on Google, you want to be on the first page. At the very least, you want to rank for your name, but better yet would be to rank for something specifically related to the books you write.

What can you do to accomplish this? Here are some tips, and a pretty straightforward guide to boosting your search rankings. These same principles apply to other businesses as well, because the point of this book is that writing is a business, and you need to treat it like one.

Most things you can do fall into three categories. The first is that your site needs to be technically accurate. The second is it needs to be full of relevant and meaningful content, and lastly, it needs to be well respected, both as a website and as a business.

Did you catch that last piece? As a business. You, as a writer, are your business, whether you write only books or articles and blog posts. I will let you in on a secret: it is easier to build authority as an expert if you also write articles and blog posts, or if you write non-fiction books along with fiction.

How do you make sure these things are true about your website? It is simpler, and yet much more work than you might think. In other words, while the solutions are simply stated, it will take a lot of work, effort, and time on your part to make your site ideal.

Analyze Your Website Technically

There is this nebulous concept called Search Engine Optimization or SEO for short. However, there are concrete steps you can take to make sure your website has the right SEO for the areas you want to rank in.

As with many of the other topics we have discussed in this series, if you don't know how to do this or don't want to take the time to learn, you should consider hiring a professional. A simple analysis and good web design are not that expensive in the long run, since your website is your home base online.

It's really like your physical store if you had one of your own. Your domain name matters as does the appearance of your website. It should look good, and the color scheme and style should be relevant to what you actually do.

The user experience, or how a user interacts with your website is like visitors at a physical location. If it is easy to move around your website, for users to find what they need, and even easy for them to buy, they will return to buy again. A website with a poor user experience is like a rude employee: it will drive customers away, and they won't ever be back.

The main difference is that in a physical store you might have one bad employee, and some customers might have a good experience. In the case of your website, you only have one employee on duty all the time, and the customer service it provides must be excellent every time.

In the case of a writer, the website experience you deliver reflects directly on you. You are your business, your store, and your only employee. Users who have a bad experience on your website might expect the same from your books.

Analyze Your Content and Create More

This step addresses two areas: technical accuracy and filling your site with relevant and meaningful content.

The first area you should already have covered: you should be an expert when it comes to your writing no matter what kind of writing you do. Whether that is fiction or non-fiction, technical or instructional, or SEO blog posts, what you share on your website should be as accurate as possible. Posts should be well researched, and state only what is known to be fact. Any guesses should be clearly stated as such.

The second part is often the trickiest for writers, especially if you create fiction. What will be most meaningful to your readers?

This can fall into a couple of categories.

Research: Often in researching fiction, we writers can become experts in some obscure subjects. Sharing that knowledge doesn't have to give away anything to your reader, but they may be fascinated by serial killers. If that is what you are writing about then after reading about your research, they may want to read more.

Setting: Where are your books set? Is it an unusual place, or somewhere many readers may not be familiar with? Is it a place you made up? Your readers will be happy to ready about it, and how you relate to that place. This is especially true if it is real, and you have fictionalized parts of it. Readers may have visited the area or may even live there and will find your perspective interesting.

You: Believe it or not, readers want to know that you, as a writer, are human. You may share your personal stories, and the exciting things you do in your daily life. You could even share your struggles, as your readers may empathize with them and feel like they know the real you.

You are your greatest asset, your greatest salesperson, and you are also the foremost expert on your characters and your writing. No one else knows them like you do and sharing that can add a great deal of value to your site and your readers' lives.

Link Building

Because you are the foremost expert on you and your writing, you can offer guest posts to other websites, including those of other authors, blog tours, and other sites with an excellent reputation.

In those posts, be sure to link back to your website at least in your bio, but even better in the body of the article or blog you write. Be sure you also link to your product pages and profile on Amazon and other sites, depending on where the blog is located, and where there readers buy most of their books. Always allow the blog to use their own affiliate links if they have them. You want them to be able to make money too.

The result of this is that your website will have a greater authority in the eyes of Google and other search engines. The more sites, especially the ones in your niche, link to your site the better. There is also a science behind keywords, and how those sites link to yours. This is a large subject, but for now it is enough to say that it is important that your deliberately build links on other sites to yours.

One of the easiest ways to do this is to trade blog posts with other authors, although this is not as effective as posting on higher authority writing sites. The reason it works at all is that quantity and quality of links both matter. Having a variety of sites that link to yours is the best practice.

This is a very rudimentary chapter about SEO, content marketing, and link building. Books have been written about each category, and you should be at least familiar with all of them.

As with many other items we discuss in this series and in the section about technical website building, if you don't know how to do these things or you feel like you don't have time to do them, you should hire an expert.

The more Google and other search engines advance, the more important it is to pay attention to these things and have a good Google ranking. This is how many new readers will find you. When it comes to marketing, this is a vital piece we will discuss in more detail in a little bit.

CHAPTER TWENTY-NINE

SEO FOR AUTHORS

"UNLESS THERE'S no rhyme or reason to your keyword research, you need to know which opportunities will take the least amount of your limited resources to yield the highest ROI."

— *Neil Patel*

"The successful person makes a habit of doing what the failing person doesn't like to do."

— *Thomas Edison*

As you start to research SEO and keywords you could become rapidly confused, especially as an author. When it comes to being a fiction author and using your website to your biggest advantage, a couple of questions you may ask yourself is what keywords should I rank for? Are my readers really searching Google for me?

The answer quite simply is yes and no. Most users start with a search for books by genre or category on Amazon until they become a fan of your work in particular that is. In this case, an author's ranking on Amazon means more than their Google ranking.

However, not all readers worldwide use Amazon, and the world is your audience. There are those who blame the demise of the book industry on the internet retail giant and won't spend money with them. There are those readers who favor iBooks, Nook, or even Kobo, which is especially popular in Europe.

Of course, all of this depends on whether you distribute your work widely or with Amazon exclusively. While the debate rages on with many authors, either way you choose to distribute, your website is what matters. Next we discuss the reasons why your website is important and what you should be ranking for.

Your Name

The first thing that matters is your name. You may think that ranking for your own name would be easy, but that is not always true. If you have a common name like Smith or Jones, there may be many people with your name in various fields. If there is someone truly famous who shares your name, this may prove to be challenging for you to rank online.

For instance, if your name is Steve King, if you type a query into Google for your name, the search engine will probably first ask you if you meant Stephen King. Even if you correct it, there are several Steve King's in the United States, and you will find rankings for many of them. In order to rank for your name, you will have to beat all of variations of it.

If you Google "Troy Lambert", I will come up high in the search and on several sites. However, there is also a Troy Lambert who is a basketball player who also ranks for same name. If he were to put effort into SEO, and I was not putting out my efforts, he could easily outrank me.

Fortunately, that is not the case. Because I participate in several blog exchanges, link build for myself intentionally, and own several websites in addition to a company of my own, my Google ranking for my name is pretty secure.

The point here is that you need to take deliberate and continuous steps to rank for your own name. If you have a business, this is true for your business name too. No matter how unique it is, you want to be number one in Google when people search for it.

Your Genre and Your Region

Ranking in your region can be easy or difficult depending on where you live and how many other authors are from your area. Ranking for your genre may be a challenge: This is especially true if you are in the romance or thriller category as both genres are rather crowded. However, if you want to rank for the "Best Romance Author" from "Your Hometown", that may be very possible.

Like any other business, local rankings matter. You should include your city and state in your bio anywhere you place it. From guest posts to your own blog to your Amazon bio, it is critical to your ranking that your name is associated with both a genre and location.

It is a fairly simple process. Your bio could read: "Troy Lambert is a suspense thriller author from Boise, Idaho." Boom. Geo-tagged.

A question is, does it really matter? The answer is a mixed one. How often does a reader search for the best author of any genre in their area? Truthfully, not often, but it does happen. Bookstores, libraries and others conduct such searches for local authors.

Conferences or schools looking for guest speakers or colleges looking for mentors may also do this type of search.

Engagements like the ones mentioned above could seriously improve your sales and propel your career. Many regional opportunities come with speaking stipends and may also boost your income.

Embracing and cultivating local notoriety and local fame is a great gig, if you can get it. While this should not be the largest focus of your marketing, its incidental side effect could be extremely beneficial when promoting your brand.

The Words Writer and Author

In any other business, it seems obvious that they would want to rank for the things that they do: Nike wants to rank for active wear and shoes, Red Bull for energy drinks, etc. However, writers are often hesitant about what they should rank for.

Take your cue from other businesses: rank for what you do. What you do is write. You are an author, and your goal is to sell books.

There is one final aspect on this SEO piece. The message of your work, fiction or non-fiction, is unique. You will want to rank for whatever your message is. One does this, in part, by paying attention to what your readers and reviewers are saying about your work and how it speaks to them. Listening to your readers will help you make appropriately focused marketing decisions.

SEO for authors is not new, it has been something authors tended to not be good about and had not pay as much attention to as they should. Still, while your ranking in Google matters and it can affect your Amazon ranking. Once you have determined what you should rank for, you may take steps to make sure your name is the first thing readers find when they search for you and your work.

CHAPTER THIRTY

A WORD ABOUT GENRE

"DON'T CLASSIFY ME, read me. I'm a writer, not a genre."

— Carlos Fuentes

"There is only one genre in fiction, the genre is called book."

— Matt Haig, The Humans

"I write across several genres. I'm a slut for words. I can't keep it in my literary pants."

— Fierce Dolan

A friend of mine often says in his talks about literature that the entire concept of genre was invented for incompetent bookseller assistants. The bookseller himself could tell you where any book on his shelves was by any author. The book assistant, though, had no idea. If a person walked in and said simply, "How do I find another book that is like this one?", the assistant would have no idea how to answer.

As the story goes, the shortcoming of the assistant would irritate the bookseller. What is the point of hiring an assistant if one had to do all the work? The solution was to group books by how they were alike: the concept of genre was born.

Since then, the concept of genre has evolved into a feature of marketing. A book's genre is the label on the shelf it would be listed under. Is that unfair? Yes, it is. Why? Because what book does not span across multiple genres? What book doesn't have elements of fantasy? When a book has more than one character, there is an higher likelihood the author may create conflict with romance. Is any of it set in space? Clearly, then the book is science fiction.

Not true? Not always, but unfortunately in the sea of books created today, there has to be a way for you to say to a reader, "This book is like these other ones." That is genre. So, what do we do about this necessary mythos that so defines our writing and our books? Branding.

Branding and What it Means

Writer's tell me all the time that they do not want to be branded. I typically ask them, "Why not? All the most successful writers are." Think about it. Stephen King, Horror. Dean Koontz, Paranormal. Tom Clancy, Technical Military Thrillers. Nicholas Sparks, Two People Almost Kiss Romance.

Branding helps readers know what to expect from your writing. They will not pick up one of your books and be surprised. Genre is the category your book fits into, the primary genre you are branded with are the kind of books readers can expect from you.

Could your brand cross genres? Yes, it can, but there will be unintentional consequences requiring you to create very clear message about the genre through the cover or with the marketing. And if you are known to write YA (young adult) books, you might want to consider using a pen name to write erotica. Employing aliases is an effective way to write across radically different genres.

How do you figure out your brand and your genre? For that, you will be required to take a closer look at your author voice.

Finding Genre

We've talked a lot about marketing in your genre, but how do you know what it is? What if your book has several elements to it? The genre is simply where you (and others on your team) think you can best market your book, nothing more than that. If a reader who associates themselves with the genre you have chosen, will they enjoy your story?

There are some things you have to consider when making these choices.

Primary Elements

If your book is set in a world where there are dragons, and the dragons and other fantastical creatures play a primary role, your book is probably fantasy. It can be a fantasy romance, an epic fantasy, or any number of sub-genres, but the primary one is fantasy.

In a romance, the plot is determined by a relationship. A mystery involves a crime or puzzle that must be solved. Science fiction usually involves a good bit of science even if it is fictionalized and is usually set in the future. You get the idea. The primary elements of your book determine the genre.

Sub-genre

The rise of sub-genres is largely due to Amazon and the perfusion of eBooks. There are dozens of sub-genres for any one genre, and they are determined by the secondary elements of your book. For instance, epic fantasy is usually defined by the scope of the world it deals with and the length of the book.

There are fine lines drawn, like the one between steamy romance and erotica. The difference is how much story verses how much the plot is tied to sex. The differences are minuscule but essential for the readers you target with your work.

Romance may be one of the pickiest genres, but others have similar constraints. Mystery has several sub-genres, as does thriller, sci-fi, and fantasy. The key is that you are aware of the constraints of each genre. Importantly, you should ensure your book meets the reader's expectations for that genre. Even if you cross sub-genres, be sure your book fits where you put it, at least according to readers.

If you don't, you may have some disappointed, angry readers. That is never going to be good for your books or your overall author branding.

The Vague Story

When should you start thinking about genre? The answer is when you start planning to write your book.

"What?" You say. "I just want to write what I want and classify it later."

That is fine except this book talks about writing as a business. As a business focused enterprise, your book should to have a target market or audience when you start writing it.

I also hear from other writers that "I write for an audience of one. Myself. I write the book I would like to read."

That's nice but here is the truth of that statement: The book you would like to read probably has a genre, and you probably have a favorite genre to both write and read. They can even be different.

"But I like to read everything."

Congratulations! So, do I, most of the time. There are exceptions, but for the most part my favorite genre is books. I tend to read more books in the genre I write, along with the related genres. I do have favorites, and the longer I write, the more I gravitate toward those favorites.

As with nearly everything in this book, there are exceptions. I know a writer who has successfully written and published in several genres. The key? In each genre, he has a specific series or set of characters who readers follow. Rarely does a one-off book that is not part of a series in a genre outside of your brand do well.

What if your story does not really fit any specific genre? You need to decide the one it resembles most closely without violating any of those genre rules, then list that as the primary genre, with others where it might fit as secondary ones.

You might not want to be branded by genre and you might not want your work to be, but it will. If you do not classify it, readers will. If they discover it.

Remember, the greatest profit is in your discoverability. Readers cannot read your books if they cannot find them, and genre is a part of that discovery process.

Next, we will talk about market spend, and what a marketing budget should look like.

CHAPTER THIRTY-ONE

HOW MUCH SHOULD I SPEND

"IT'S WAITING that helps you as an investor, and a lot of people can't stand to wait. If you did not get that deferred gratification gene, you've got work very hard to overcome that. "

--Charles Munger

"Marketing is really just about sharing your passion."

-–Michael Hyatt,

"Nobody counts the number of ads you run; they just remember the impression you make."

-–Bill Bernbach

"Doing business without advertising is like winking at a girl in the dark. You know what you are doing, but nobody else does."

-–Steuart Henderson Britt

If that last quote does not hit home for you, read it again. The point of this book, and specifically this section, is that writing is both a business and a passion: without embracing the business portion of it, you likely won't get anywhere, at least if you want to do this for a living. You must put money into your own business. We covered in production how to invest in editing, covers, and formatting.

You must invest in distributing your books, but often your biggest expense will be marketing. So how do you decide how much to invest? There are a few steps necessary for you to decide, and you must follow them systematically.

Remember back to the beginning of this book when we said that your book, once finished, is a product you must sell. This requires you to approach how much you spend on marketing the same way any successful business would approach marketing any other product or service.

Initial Spending

Anyone who is worth their salt as a marketer will tell you that you need to spend a lot out of the gate to launch a product. Remember what we said about discoverability? That is all contingent on ad spend. It is especially true if you are a new author: you do not have enough fans or friends to sell enough books to make a living requiring you to pay for word of mouth about your books. This is called advertising.

Part of advertising is marketing your book through social media, which includes paid ads, Amazon ads, Bookbub ads, and in some cases even Google PPC ads.

To determine how much all this will cost, we must first answer some other questions first.

Testing

How do you know what is working? You need to test your ads at first. First, create a few ads then test them on each platform. Some platforms have programs to help you test your ads. The reason being is platforms want you to keep marketing with them and the best way to do this is to make their platform user-friendly and flexible to their customer's needs.

Often platforms, like Facebook and Amazon, will give you the option to display only your best performing ads along with automatically promoting what is working. This can be good: It gives you the flexibility to stop ads that are less effective and increase spending on those that are in addition to create new ads to test. The more you rotate your ads, the more you will learn about what will work for you.

Once you have the ads that work best established, which includes the ads that get the most clicks and the ones that get the most sales, you may then concentrate your spend on these ads.

Setting an Ongoing Marketing Budget

Just as with other products, no author should advertise their books just once with one go at marketing then thing they are done. You need to keep working at it by evaluating and concentrating on a few things:

- What is your ROI on each ad and each platform? Are you not only making your investment back but then some?
- How often do you put your book on sale? This is a common question. You make less money per sale when your price is reduced, but you also have more sales. Still, if you put your book on sale too often, readers will rarely

pay full price for your books. They will simply wait until prices are lower. There is a balance with this process.

- How much can you afford? Seriously, this is a real concern. Marketing, while it can be data driven, is somewhat of a gamble. You could lose your money with nothing in return or lose money on your marketing efforts. As a rule, don't gamble with the rent or mortgage money but spend what you can on marketing. For a business that is profitable, this is usually tied to a percentage of that profit, somewhere in the 30% range. Until you are profitable though, you will have to invest more than that it most cases.

You should budget and plan for your marketing efforts in order to make a living as an author. As with any other business, one must spend money to make money.

If your marketing budget is below a few hundred dollars a month, you are probably spending too little. If you are losing money every month, you are probably spending too much without adequate testing.

This brings us to one of the main themes of this book: when is it time to hire the pros?

CHAPTER THIRTY-TWO

TIME IS MONEY: HIRING HELP

I CHOOSE a lazy person to do a hard job. Because a lazy person will find an easy way to do it.

--Bill Gates

I hire people brighter than me and then I get out of their way.

--Lee Iacocca

Find ballplayers, not those who look good in baseball caps.

--Tom Monahan, CEB

The constant debate with many authors, especially indie authors, is when it makes sense to hire help. In large part, this is about budget: I cannot understate, if you do not have a budget for hiring others in every stage of the process, your business will not be as healthy as it could be.

When you hire help, though, it is obviously more expensive than doing things yourself or having someone you know help you or do it for you. However, unless you are a marketing expert, or your wife or kids are, a pro will already know what works and what doesn't and will have to do less testing. A marketing professional will likely secure better results than you would on your own.

While your initial output may be greater; in the long run, you may spend less on marketing by hiring a pro. How do you know when it is time? What help do you need that you can afford?

Start with Marketing

Marketing and advertising require a lot of time, attention, and effort. These are probably areas you probably do not excel in or even enjoy doing.

As asserted earlier, you may save money and make more money in the long run by hiring a pro to handle at least some of your marketing work for you. Often the pros will guarantee results or at least offer some assurances their methods will work.

The kind of marketing do you hire out largely depends on your goals. Hire someone to do several things to include some of the following public relations and ad management functions:

- Increase your email subscribers: There are services and PR companies who will employ specific strategies and contests to entice subscribers to join your list.
- Increase Amazon Author Page followers and optimize your Amazon Author central page
- Increase Facebook likes and Group Members
- Increase Book Bub followers

- Increase Goodreads followers and optimize your Goodreads presence
- Handle your newsletter publication and optimization
- Manage ads on Facebook, Amazon, Bookbub, and elsewhere.
- Help you set up blog tours, podcast and TV interviews, radio interviews, and more.

Some of campaigns you may do yourself. Some you could delegate to a VA (virtual assistant) who will help you with administrative tasks.

The positive affect is that this frees you up to write more, so you may write faster as we discussed in the first section of this book. The more often you release or churn something out the more Amazon will recognize your name, and this productivity will create more automatic advertising of your brand. With more creations to market and advertise, you will be able to make more money.

Hiring marketing pros is just step one though. There are also other areas of a business where one could and should hire a team.

Social Media Management

Social media management may be outsourced and even a portion of it automated. There are actually two different steps in this process.

- **Business Process Automation:** You have probably heard this term when it comes to other businesses, but it also applies to the writing business too, especially social media. While you do need to be present from time to time to add the personal touch to your social media. So that your only communication with your followers are not just blasts of buy my book, automate at least some posts that belong to others.

- **Social Media Administrators:** These professionals handle many of your social media postings for you, search for relevant content, and put it on your page for you. They also will help you respond to messages and comments, keeping the time you spend on social media to a minimum.

Yes, in the long run you need to be present and handling your social media platforms, but you can get help. Automation and administrators are two of the best ways to save yourself time.

Administration and Accounting

This entire book is about writing as a business, and in order for that to work, you should be able to employ some basic administration and accounting functions. Another very important time when writers require additional help is during tax season: knowing what you can and cannot write off plus having an understanding your business's standard deductions are some of the key barriers writers face.

The other part of this equation is that usually writers are not the greatest businesspeople. Creatives tend to be better with words, art, music, or other endeavors where their imagination is free to run wild. However, for a successful business, it is best not to be creative with your accounting practices. Doing so will likely to sink your business and get you in real legal trouble too.

Again, there are exceptions to the rule; there are writers who are also good at accounting and math. They tend to be the exception though. Often writers have a spouse or partner who is good at the accounting side of the business (opposites often attract), so they handle the financial part or least help with it.

Administrative tasks are things that take time and effort for a writer who otherwise could be writing. Beyond handling money, ads must be designed and posted, correspondence must be answered, and all this in addition to basic and ongoing communication between the writer's business and their publishers, editors, cover designers, reviewers, and customers. Books must be sent out for reviews or to satisfy contest winners.

A writer may require an assistant to administer and update their website, keep the blog current, handle writing inquiries, and manage their calendar. Calendar management may include but is certainly not limited to setting up appearances at conferences, book signings, workshops, or business meetings.

These are all tasks someone else can do for you, and probably do more efficiently. There are those who enjoy those tasks and using them just makes sense. Understand that these are professionals you must pay. If you use your friends and family, there can be some frustration when they don't follow through and you have to do things yourself. Someone you pay is someone you can also hold accountable to make sure things are getting done.

Public Relations

We will talk about this in more depth the next section but here we touch on public relations as a function of discoverability. Making sure people can find you and your work is really important and has a big impact on your bottom line. In today's market, often readers want to know you and feel they can relate to you, the writer.

Brand building and the illusion of accessibility are managed through your public image via public relations. Things like conference appearances, speaking engagements, speaking at schools and to college classes, appearing in libraries, holding book signings, and a myriad of other public activities are key to your writing career.

"But I am an introvert!" you exclaim loudly. So are most writers. You will have to suck it up and do whatever you need to do to overcome the inclination to isolate. Podcasts, blogs, vlogs, and other activities will require you to be out of your comfort zone. I cannot stress more strongly that you will always be the best spokesman for your books, as you wrote them and know the characters better than anyone else ever will.

However, scheduling all of those things is a challenge, especially for most creative introvert who just wants to show up and do their thing. So, hiring a PR firm to help you with at least some of those things just makes sense. There is a cost associated with farming out convenience: PR firms will either require an upfront payment or take a percentage of your book sales or speaking fees. That is part of the deal to becoming discoverable; more exposure generates greater income.

The other aspect of hiring a PR firm is that they know your niche and your market. They know what works and what doesn't, what conferences you should attend or skip, as well as where your work will have a greater likelihood of generating income and promoting the best exposure.

Personal Tasks

There are all kinds of distractions for a writer, especially if you work at home and write full time. Things like yard work, walking the dog, picking up the poop or cleaning the litter box, laundry, house cleaning, and more can, and will all detract from your writing time, if you allow it to.

If you are like most full-time writers, you cannot afford to outsource all home maintenance tasks, but you may be able to afford a few services that will help you maximize your time better. While you may enjoy at least some of those things as they offer you a chance to take a break, be careful that they are not an excuse to avoid your writing work. If you are able to outsource them, have your kids to help, or schedule them outside of your writing time, every little bit helps when safeguarding your writing time as productive writing time.

Hiring help does one thing: it helps you concentrate on the part of your business you are best at: writing and creating. Anything you can do to produce more, the better. Help with the end of the production process, distribution, and marketing are all ways to make yourself a better and more successful writer.

CHAPTER THIRTY-THREE

THE ADVANTAGE OF THE PROS

SELF-CARE IS NEVER a selfish act - it is simply good steward-ship of the only gift I have, the gift I was put on earth to offer others. Anytime we can listen to true self and give the care it requires, we do it not only for ourselves, but for the many others whose lives we touch.

— Parker Palmer, Let Your Life Speak: Listening for the Voice of Vocation

The other part of outsourcing is this: it simply says where the work can be done outside better than it can be done inside, we should do it.

—Alphonso Jackson

I hope that you understand after the last chapter in addition to the other things we had discussed in the sections on production and distribution, it simply makes sense to hire a pro to do many of the things you either don't know how to do, are not the best at, or you just don't have time for.

It is important to stress that you decide what you want to focus on. As a writer you are a professional storyteller. You are in the business of telling your story, helping a business tell a story about a product, or creating a screenplay. Whatever you are doing with regard to writing, make sure you are the professional.

This could mean you are really good at marketing and social media, and that you like doing this type of work. That can be a big advantage, because the writers who are good at that kind of thing are few and far between. Even so, you should evaluate how you are spending your time, and how that time spent is money.

Let's look at some examples on how to determine your ROI. A caveat before we start: deciding which tasks to outsource is about more than money. It can be about what you enjoy and how it relates to what you can and cannot do when it comes to the business side of writing.

Time is Money

We said this before, but it is time to break it down with some specific examples. Let's say that you have a deadline for a book; that book is for you to self-publish or for a publisher to publish. The reason you have the deadline is the book is seasonal: maybe it is set at Christmas and will only really sell for a few months in the year. Maybe the book was slated to be part of a summer reads program and should hit the shelves before kids are out of school for the summer.

If you miss your deadline because you were marketing one of your current works or revising another book that does not have as tight of a deadline, your book may not be out in time for the target season resulting in potential loss of sales.

If you have that book accepted by a publisher, they may cancel your contract, costing you time and money to shop it to other publishers. The point is, that time would have been better spent writing and reaching your deadline than marketing. At the same time, you did not want the marketing to stop. Hiring a marketing professional would have helped you reach both goals: writing and staying current with your marketing plan.

There are countless other examples: Time spent on social media is another one. Trying to design a cover is another. Each task mentioned above, from accounting to administration can be seen as a waste of your creative time when you could be writing faster (see the first section of this book) and producing more.

Stress Kills Creativity

Does accounting stress you out? How about uploading your book to all of those marketing sites we talked about? Making sure you have it in multiple formats? What about interior formatting? Are these tasks you just really don't want to do?

The truth is, the more time you spend on the tasks you like least, the less time you have to write, and that, itself, may cause stress. There are some tasks that have nothing to do with time. They may simply be in areas where you don't have the skills you need, so you are learning as you go or are just struggling with developing skills you are not adept at: This will stress you out.

Many authors, and, frankly, many entrepreneurs are not good with numbers. One of the first tasks they outsource is accounting, and one primary reason is stress. I do assert you should know enough about your business to have a basic grasp of what is going on with your accounting, but actually doing the books is probably a waste of your time and energy.

Look back at everything we have covered in this book so far. Does just looking at the list stress you out? If it doesn't, it probably should. Being skilled enough to personally do every aspect of your business while maintaining your creative edge is very difficult and will become a major strain on your personal health, your creative resources, and the health of your business. Once you have experienced a certain amount of growth and your business reaches certain critical size, doing all business-related tasks will become impossible for one person to manage.

That stress will rob you of your creativity. Writers will often say, "I just don't have headspace for all of that." They are right. No one does. Let the pros be pros and take that stress off your shoulders.

Quality Suffers

You are more likely to make a mistake in your financial books than your accountant. You may not have the expertise to test the right things when it comes to marketing. Your ads may not be as good as a professional advertiser.

This is especially true when it comes to the production side of things; i.e., formatting, covers, and the various other tasks you are required to perform. You may be able to do it and do a good-enough job, but a professional cover designer will do an excellent job while keeping costs fairly low in comparison to the time it may have taken away from your writing to do it yourself.

You want your brand and your business to be known for excellence, not just "good" or "good enough". The solution? Hire the pros in those areas where you are the least skilled.

Self-Care

You are a good writer, maybe even a great one. Specialize and concentrate on what you are a pro at doing then outsource the rest of the tasks on your to-do list. Invest money in yourself and your self-care. Eat healthy, exercise, get adequate sleep, and nurture your relationships while you pursue your dream and writing as a business.

Think of self-care like any other job. If you are gone too much, overworked, or constantly tired, you will not function at one hundred percent. This is your livelihood: it is your writing and your stories. Top level functioning is really the real-world standard, and the only way one can manage to reach that benchmark is to take care of oneself.

There are a lot of advantages when the professional writer uses the pros, but the most important is in order for your writing business to prosper, you should be willing to outsource, let go of some transactional control, and spend your time and energy doing what you do best, writing.

In the next chapter, we will touch on physical book marketing, and how you can turn those very expensive business cards into a profitable arm of your business whether you write fiction or non-fiction.

CHAPTER THIRTY-FOUR

SOME NOTES ON PHYSICAL BOOK MARKETING

IF YOU DROP a book into the toilet, you can fish it out, dry it off and read that book. But if you drop your Kindle in the toilet, you're pretty well done.

—Stephen King

Stock complaints about the inherent pleasure of ye olde format are bandied about whenever some new upstart invention comes along. Each moan is nothing more than a little fetus of nostalgia jerking in your gut.

— Charlie Brooker

As long as there have been eBooks there has been a debate about which is superior, print or digital. The Kindle and other reading devices allow you to take books nearly anywhere —hundreds of them allowing you to have a library in your pocket.

Sounds like a book lovers dream, right? Then why are so many book lovers so adamantly opposed to reading digitally? Yes, you have to charge your ereader, but if you wish you can read with apps on your phone, on your computer, or on nearly any other electronic device. Digital books make reading, and reading anywhere, easier than it has ever been.

What about from an author perspective though? What is the eBook revolution doing to the business of writing, and how do print books and print book marketing fit in? Earlier in this book, we discussed print books as a function of distribution, but what does this look like from the viewpoint of marketing?

The essential thing is this: if you are going to have print books, you need to market them as a part of your product line. Think of print books as a calling card; print books are a really expensive business card. As a tactile advertisement, print books can work to boost digital sales.

So, what does that marketing for physical books look like? For us to explore that, we need to look back at some of the things we discussed back in the section on distribution then touch a bit on production.

Libraries and Bookstores

The two best places for print books to be found are libraries and bookstores. If you have non-fiction outdoor guides, photography books, or other books that relate to certain hobbies and retail outlets (like cookbooks) then there will be other avenues, but the audience is somewhat different than that for fiction books.

In other words, if you offer hiking guides for specific regional areas, you will probably have an audience of hikers that may or may not read other types of books. This group of readers will be more likely to spot your book at REI or another outdoor outlet rather than at Barnes and Noble. They are also more likely to want to purchase their own copy, in print, rather than borrow it from a library or have it in eBook form, especially when they are hiking in the woods where there is no power (unless they are carrying solar chargers, a cool but unrelated argument unrelated to this book).

Fiction authors are most likely to find their print book in the library and the bookstore. Earlier in this book, we touched a bit on distribution to these outlets and working with indie bookstores as an indie author. Likewise, it is necessary to touch on that just a little bit more here under marketing.

Who Prints Your Books?

For many indie authors, Create Space, an arm of Amazon that has now merged with their KDP platform, allows authors to offer print books on demand (no paying for huge print runs) and it is pretty easy to set up and order from. As discussed before, a pro will be required to design a cover and format the book's interior, or you will need to learn to do your own formatting really well and quickly.

There are programs that help you create eBooks and even print files for the interior of your book, and if you are a Mac user, I highly suggest Vellum, an extremely valuable and relatively inexpensive software that does much of the work for you. You'll still have to pay attention to settings, and illustrations and graphs still pose unique challenges in non-fiction, but the process is much faster once you master the program.

There are a couple of issues with this when it comes to bookstores and libraries though. Many indie bookstores will not order books from Amazon: having a driver deliver an Amazon box to their bookstore is like someone at Pizza Hut getting a delivery from

Domino's while they are on the clock. They won't do it. Many of their customers would be appalled.

How do they get your books then? Of course, you have an ISBN (you do, right?) so they could order it through Ingram if you have it listed there but be warned: if your ISBN is not tied to you, the publisher, but is a free, Amazon one, you may still have trouble with distribution, and you will make less money. Not only does Amazon take their cut, Ingram also purchases them at a discount, so you will not make a lot of money per print copy.

The other option an author has is to go with Ingram Spark or another similar program. This offers several advantages and does avoid the stigma associated with Amazon; by taking advantage of the cons of wide distribution, the author is not putting all their eggs in the same basket. Your print distribution is entirely separate from your eBook platform on Amazon.

Many authors now have taken to creating two print versions of their book now, one for Amazon and one for Ingram. This satisfies the bookstores and libraries and wider print distribution, but it also helps sales on Amazon, where they tend to promote the print books created in KDP. Also, even if Amazon lists your Ingram print book, they usually list it with low quantities on hand and long delivery times, information that, while not always accurate, can discourage buyers. This means you'll have to create two cover files to meet the requirements of both platforms, but typically your cover designer can do that for you at little or no extra cost.

It also makes it easier for bookstores and libraries, especially those out of your area, to find, order, and carry your books. Making sure your books are available in the more traditional acquisition channels, helps you market your books to a wider audience. It's still print-on-demand (POD), and the cost is still affordable, but when other outlets buy your book you don't make as much profit as when you sell author copies yourself. However, you will likely sell more copies if you market your print books correctly, and that is part of what we will talk about next.

Back of the Buick and Garage Distribution Method

Many indie authors, intimidated by the traditional printing systems or the cost of print runs, opt instead for back of Buick and my garage distribution methods. You simply order your author copies from Amazon or Ingram and drive them around or ship them to outlets that want to carry them. This way you keep all of the profits, right? You can even sell them on your website with a significant margin.

There are several reasons why this may not work to an author's advantage. While we have discussed them already in the distribution section of this book, let's touch them again here.

- **A Limited Audience:** Rather than just finding your book in a catalog or being able to order it from anywhere, the bookstore or library has to find you or your website. What if they don't know you, or they do not discover you and your book in some other way? They will never order your books.
- **The Time Suck:** It's much easier to send an outreach letter to library systems, both local and around the country, with your ISBN and invite them to order and carry your book than it is to contact them individually then offer them a way to order direct from you. Worth mentioning here is many libraries and bookstores don't have an invoicing and POS system that enables them to purchase directly from the author.
- **Be a Pro:** Professional authors don't set things up this way. We have distribution channels for a reason, with

one of them being a concerted professional marketing approach that works in tandem with the system bookstores and libraries are comfortable working with. Want to be perceived as a pro? Market like one.

Remember what we said about hiring pros? A marketing and PR firm will not want to contact you or refer their contacts directly to you to purchase your print books. They should be able to, but that is usually not their first option or preferred method. Besides, you do not have time to manage the distribution of your print books: remember, you are working; writing more and faster with the primary focus of building your business.

Look, if you are going to have print books, you need to market them like the professional you are. Yes, it can still be hard to get them in bookstores and libraries in areas where you are not well known. The key is to follow all of the steps we've discussed here to become known. The wider you and your books are known, the more clout you have in larger markets and the easier it will be to market your work.

Book Signings and Events

We're actually going to devote a whole chapter to this next. This is one of the best and one of the worst ways to market books, but the next chapter addresses the pros and cons while highlighting how you, the professional, will make these methods work for you.

CHAPTER THIRTY-FIVE

BOOK SIGNINGS, TOURS, AND EVENTS

I REMEMBER the days of sitting at book signings, playing with my pen when no one would come, and still I even then thought I was living the dream, because I had a book out.

—Harlan Coben

There are other types of public appearances a writer does in addition to book signings and readings. Each calls for different skills. None of these skills, needless to say, are those that go into writing books.

—Jane Lindskold

I wonder what book signings will be like when most of the books we read are electronic. Will authors sign something else? A flyer, perhaps? A special kind of card devised for the purpose?

—Susan Orlean

One aspect of book marketing often neglected by indie authors is book signings, tours, and other events. Why is this? Quite simply, these methods often don't pay off. The author may sit for hours, with no one in store stopping to say hello, let alone buy a book or ask for a signature.

In fact, this often used to be a tactic for book publishers. A young author, with a tiny following, would ask for a book tour to boost sales, and the PR people would say yes, although the author was required to pay much of their own expenses.

"Send them on the lonely, empty bookstore tour," they would say. By only a short way in, the writer would be discouraged, and often even blame the publisher.

"I show up at these events, and no one comes, no one buys any books," they say. Is the fault in the bookstore and the publisher, and how much they promote the event, or is the fault with the author? The answer is, quite simply, both. Let's explore some aspects of these things, and other types of events, in more detail.

The Bookstore Signing

Bookstore signing events has been the bread and butter of many top selling authors and even those in the middle of the rankings. It is tougher today for a number of reasons. Still, bookstore signings can be very lucrative with the following caveats:

- **Start with local bookstores.** You will have more of a following locally, and more local people will be curious about a local author rather than one outside of their region. Additionally, you probably have a better relationship with your local bookstore than one farther away.
- **Become known.** Local awards are free advertising

that could help build and create name-recognition of your brand locally. They also tend to mean a lot in your local bookstore and your community. These opportunities could be in the form of a feature article by the local paper or a spot on the local news station; market to anyone who will listen to your story and let you tell it publicly.

- **Use your network to expand.** You know authors in other cities and other markets. Enlist their help in spreading the word about your book and your work before you come to their region: likewise, building networks is part of getting your name out beyond your local city so offer to do the same for them when they come to your area. Work together, get introductions to local bookstore owners, and use your local events to prove you have a draw.

- **Plan to stay awhile.** Often authors stay only a short time at bookstores and get angry when no one shows up. Even if you have an event in the evening, show up early. Hang around with the staff. Talk to readers. Offer to help them rather than just taking up space. If your event is earlier in the day, plan to stay as long as you can. Network and talk to readers as much as you can.

- **Understand things you can't control.** If you are in a Seattle bookstore, and it is a rare sunny day, don't expect a lot of foot traffic. If you are in the Midwest during tornado season, don't expect a huge evening turnout.

- **Manage expectations.** Not every bookstore signing is created equally. Some will do better than others. That's just a fact. Accept it, be grateful for even meeting one reader or five, but never get angry, resentful, or even hostile. You will likely never be invited back, even when you have a more established name.

Remember, you are a pro. That is the point of all this work you are putting in. Even Babe Ruth did not hit a home run every at bat, and you're bound to strike out from time to time. You'll have great signings, and you will have mediocre ones: Take the good with the bad but take it either way with grace.

Library Signings

Understand one thing about libraries. Outside of events (more on that in a second) people generally do not come to the library with money, ready to buy books. They come to borrow them for free. This said, often "meet the author" and library signings do not yield a lot of sales.

The solution is to have an author talk and an event rather than just a signing where you sit at a table with a stack of your books. Many libraries are headed this way anyway. With the onslaught of eBooks, their role within the community they serve is changing dramatically from the libraries of old. In addition to lending books, movies, and even music, libraries have become community centers with events, workspaces, education, and more.

So, how do authors host a library event that yields maximum, yet mutual benefit? Libraries and authors have all kinds of collaborative solutions.

- Invite multiple authors at the same time.
- Do a talk about your book or the topic of your book.
- Have a workshop or other event.
- Hold a contest and announce the winners at the event.
- Have a local author award of some sort and have a

reception to announce the winner.

- Run a comic con or a book con by genre or theme.

These are just a few examples. Libraries and authors are coming up with all kinds of innovative ways to excite readers and nonreaders alike by promoting libraries as places to meet and utilize services while introducing authors from all over the country who specialize in a broad range of genres. Get to know your local librarian. Get to know librarians in the cities you will travel to. Done right, enlisting area libraries to foster and promote professional networking opportunities could result in highly respectful collaborations that promote your brand and other authors in a way that benefits you, the author, but also the communities you extend your reach to.

Conventions and other Events

Here is the skinny on conventions or cons, as they are commonly and affectionately called by insiders. Unless you have a book written for writers, a writer's conference is a great opportunity to learn and to network, but you may not sell as many books as you would like. The reason being is authors are inundated with their friends' books, other authors who want them to review their books, and yet other authors are focused on promoting their own writing.

Authors like to read, and we also often like to buy books, but your target audience is really the average reader. This means reader focused conventions or at least cons that have reader focused events are where you will have greater sales opportunities.

Even if you do not write sci-fi and fantasy, comic cons and other conventions can be a good place to sell books. Attendees tend to embrace indie works, and many read romance, mystery, horror, and other genres.

Other events such as book fairs and book festivals held in many cities are good sales opportunities, especially if they reach large reader groups and focus primarily on reader events. Remember, it is partly about ROI and partly about becoming known by building a recognizable author brand in an area or in a genre. It is perfectly acceptable to work these types of events for exposure as much as it is for the money.

Tips and Tricks

With all of the authors and events out there, how do you make yours stand out? It is an appropriate question, and below are a few ways authors make the most of attending a con or other such events. Besides knowing the location and the audience you are reaching, there are some common book marketing ideas that really boost sales.

- Hold an event or party, not just a signing.
- Do something unusual. Have a readers' theater production of part of your book. Have a contest or host a Q and A about some of your research.
- Have freebies and giveaways. Cookies and treats, coffee, pens you sign books with, coupons, drink tickets, and other swag all work. Anything you as a reader would love, your readers will love too.
- Be a panelist or petition a con's leadership to host a workshop or reading during the con; this will be heavily dependent on your genre and professional level of expertise. It will also require a bit of planning, networking, and preparation. In any case, participation at cons is a great way to build recognition, represent your author brand and to become considered an authority by fostering influence within the trade.
- Sign stuff other than books. Unless your publisher forbids

it, have posters, cards, bookmarks, and even merchandise to sign for those who read eBooks but still want to meet you and would like you to sign something. If you are at a bookstore, be sure you encourage book purchases, and if you do sell swag, give the bookstore a cut of the merchandise profits.

- Market, market, market. Yes, it is the bookstore's job to market their events, but it is yours too. Remember, use your network, offer tickets, event specials, and other ways to attract readers.

Think of the last book signing or book event you went to. Why did you go to that one in particular? What drew you to it? How successful was it? How was it structured?

Those things that attracted you will attract others too. Be creative in your marketing and your events in the same way you are with your books.

Next, we will wrap up the marketing section and then add some final words to try to pull all of this information together.

CHAPTER THIRTY-SIX

YOUR MARKETING PLAN (S}

"WHATEVER THE STATUS QUO IS, changing it gives you the opportunity to be remarkable."

--*Seth Godin*

"Marketing strategy will impact every piece of your business and it should be tied to every piece of your business."

--*Brandon Andersen, Chief Strategist of Cardlytics*

Summing up all of this information on marketing you now have, if it isn't applied, it is rendered useless. So, how do we take all of this information and apply it? The answer is in developing a marketing plan.

There are marketing templates online, and you could and should download them and become comfortable utilizing the various formats. Below we will review two types of plans and what they include.

The Two Marketing Plans

There are two types of marketing plans. One is for you, the writer, and your overall brand. The other is for each individual book you release. Think of it this way. Toyota is an automotive brand, and they want to be associated with a certain type and feel of car and truck. That is their branding. They have a logo that appears on each car and each ad, all of which subscribe to a certain look and feel.

However, Toyota also has several cars, trucks, and SUVs, and they have marketing plans and campaigns for each of those that combine with their overall brand. Each one has a certain look, feel, performance, and price range. Toyota has a high-end, luxury arm of the brand, Lexus.

As a writer, you are a brand. Your name is your logo. The genre you are currently writing in or write in most of the time is also a part of your brand. Additionally, your brand includes all of your book covers, especially those in a series since each maintain the same type of look and feel. All this defines you.

However, each book also has their own particular characteristics and appeal for a specific audience. Authors need to market those as well: if one just markets their brand without consideration for the individual book's characteristics and its audience, missed opportunities will result because readers will wonder which books they will like and should buy.

It is up to the author to market both, so a marketing plan is required for both. Your brand is the constant. The books you spend most of your marketing dollars on vary depending on what you have published most recently, and which are your most popular books.

Budget

Each of your marketing plans should have a budget. The one for you, the author, will be ongoing. The one for your books will vary as the book age out, but there should be a consistent amount for two categories: current releases and your backlist. As mentioned in an earlier chapter, how much you should spend largely depends on you. However, the more you invest in your work, the greater your return will be.

Goals and a Timeline

Each of your campaigns should have a timeline and goals. How do you know if you are succeeding if you don't have something you are aiming for? This could be a goal of sales or a goal of profit or a two-pronged goal to see increases in both. Your marketing campaign should also have a timeline. You could (and should) have more than one campaign per marketing plan and timelines for each that overlap.

The key is writing professionals must have something to measure or some way to determine ROI in order to know which campaigns work best. Even if you hire professionals, for the health of your business you should review these plans with your marketing team routinely to set and manage expectations by enlisting your goals as benchmarks to ensure marketing efforts are working in a way that is paying off for your business.

Measuring Tools

Thanks to analytics and all kinds of online tools, astute business-people measure what is working and what is not when it comes to marketing plans and campaigns. To see the benefit of analytical tools, here are some things you should be measuring.

- Sales and download numbers: How many people are buying your work during a campaign?
- Profit and loss: If you mark your book down to 0.99 for a sale, that means you are making less royalty per sale. Be sure you are figuring out your ROI using the right set of numbers to figure out your profit.
- Amazon rankings: Amazon rankings are based as much on visits to your book page, reviews, and a few other nuanced proprietary things. Watch how marketing campaigns move those rankings and use that to help measure the value of each one.
- ACOS: This is something called Average Cost of Sale, and is an advanced marketing technique to determine ROI. It is usually expressed as a percentage. Research it, learn about how it works, and even set goals in this area.

It is no good to have goals unless you are measuring to see if you are achieving them, and we have a lot of modern tools to help us do just that. Use them or have your marketing team use them, but for either scenario, ensure you are evaluating outcomes of marketing efforts and adjusting accordingly.

Reporting

Give marketing efforts time to work, as not every campaign yields instant results. But you do need to routinely review overall trends ensuring marketing efforts are yielding desired results. This means each a month you are conducting a review of sales, author rankings, book rankings, and profits for that month.

Also, as a book ages, ensure you are cultivating overall brand health and steady sales by writing more and by releasing more work. If you're not, only so much marketing of your old work will result in continued sales. The professional writer's rule of thumb is don't stop producing, and no matter what the reports say, don't ever stop marketing either.

Evaluation and Contingency

No one wants to throw away good money on things that are not working. Be open to adjusting the market approache for each book until you find a mix that works best for that particular title.

For instance, LinkedIn ads could be a real winner for non-fiction books or business books because LinkedIn is where businesspeople hang out, and where these genres are likely to find readers or a network of peers. Amazon ads may be equally effective, but one or the other effort might win out over the other. By reviewing marketing reports and following a concerted marketing plan and strategy, savvy business professionals shift marketing dollars to the channel that works best.

For fiction, often one social media platform will work better than others. Amazon ads may also work well, if they are structured and tested correctly. The idea is to do the same thing—invest the marketing budget for a campaign where it is reaping the most good. Divorce emotion from the decision as much as possible. This is not about what you want to work, what you hope would work, but what actually does work.

Struggling with a particular book's marketing plan? Have a contingency plan and reevaluate. As always, if you just can't get anything to work, try calling in the pros, at the very least to consult with them: your job is to be a writer, and their expertise lies in marketing. Let the pros do what they do best, and if you must do it yourself, become a pro at it.

There are marketing plan templates and there are those who can help you write them if you have trouble or just don't have the time. In either case, you must understand them and have a plan with it as an integral part of your overall writing business plan.

There is a ton to do, and not enough time to do it all. How you hire and structure your team will largely depend on how many books you have out, whether you are still working a day job, and what free assistance you can find. Marketing is time consuming and often frustrating; these qualities makes it one of the best areas of your business to hire help for.

Have we covered everything about marketing and marketing plans for books? Not really. That requires an entire book on just that subject alone, and such books are already out there. The key is to be aware of the necessity of marketing and the basic framework of a marketing plan. You can research more in depth from there.

Finally, next let's look at how to pull the whole book together and set yourself up for writing success.

CONCLUSION: THE END AND THE BEGINNING

"WHEN A WRITER IS BORN into a family, the family is finished."

— Czeslaw Milosz

"Who wants to become a writer? And why? Because it's the answer to everything. ... It's the streaming reason for living. To note, to pin down, to build up, to create, to be astonished at nothing, to cherish the oddities, to let nothing go down the drain, to make something, to make a great flower out of life, even if it's a cactus."

—Enid Bagnold

We've come a long way since the start of this book. By the time you read it, some specific examples highlighted in these pages or pixels may have already experienced some change. However, the overall principles will remain the same, because writing is a business. The professional author must engage in production, distribute their work, and market it just like one would if they created a new video game, recorded a song, or developed the next flavor of ice cream.

When it comes down to it, books are products for sale, and just like any other business, there are steps to go with that. Quality matters. Know your audience and reach them where they are at the right time. We've come to a few concrete conclusions in this book, but there are some areas that remain vague, high level constructs. There is a reason for that. Not everything works for every writer, and there are exceptions to every rule. However, let's review really quickly the main concepts covered.

- You have to produce work in order to sell it. This means writing consistently and at a reasonable pace, so your readers always have something you created to consume.
- A part of production includes editing, covers, formatting, and more. To do this well, and the right way, requires a team.
- For people to find your work, it must be distributed somewhere. In most cases, wide distribution in multiple formats is the answer. Those formats may change over time.
- Once your book is distributed well, you need to market it. Your number one struggle will always be discoverability, and marketing is the answer to that struggle.

How should you use this book? The first time, you should probably have read it all the way through, just like I recommended at the beginning. Then you can go back and review sections as need be, depending on where you are in your business journey.

Other Advice

This book could not cover every aspect of writing as a business. There are other things like accounting, determining cash flow, taxes and what deductions are actually legal, details on copyright laws, and other parts of the business that truly do matter to your success and profitability.

Recall, the key is if you have written a book, you are an entrepreneur. You need a business plan, a financial plan that includes funding, a marketing plan, along with the nuanced things mentioned in the above paragraph to succeed by writing as a business. Writing for a living is hard, and it means you need more than one stream of income and a plan for how to make ends meet.

You'll need a network of cohorts. A community of entrepreneurial writers who are available to talk through the tough, lean times, learn from, and celebrate successes. It is a collaborative community where relationships offer emotional support, trade experiences, and field suggestions for cultivating a team of outsourced professionals to help you through with the various stages of your business. As the CEO and the talent for your organization, you can't do it all on your own.

Read about both the craft of your writing and the business side of being a professional writer. If you want to make a living writing this is essential. Read in your genre and outside of it too. Hire pros, not just to help you do things right, but ensure you maintain a work-life balance by making time for your family and by cultivating other interests and hobbies: this will not only make your life more interesting and worth living but will make what you write more innovative when you invest in refueling your creative bucket.

Take care of yourself physically. It is difficult for us writers whose jobs are essentially sedentary. Work out. Hike, bike, get outside and explore.

Writing is a business. It consists of production, distribution, and marketing. While the principles are simple, the application is much more challenging. If you choose to embark on this journey understand it is both awful and awesome. Most of the time, the awesome outweighs the rest.

Writers happen to the best of families, despite the best of intentions. If you're like me, and otherwise unskilled and unemployable, being a writer is the greatest thing ever, and making a living from it is extremely gratifying. To make it a success, you're going to have to treat it like any other business. For the creatives in us, that is the greatest challenge of all. I hope this book helps you as it helped me.

Write on. I can't wait to see how far you will go. This may be the end of this book, but it's only the beginning of your writing journey.

THE END

OTHER RESOURCES

THERE ARE a ton of books and resources out there when it comes to writing as a business, and it is impossible to list all of them. However, here are a few key things to read and study. If you are reading this book digitally, there are links below. If you are reading it in print, simply search for the resources by name.

Rand Fishkin, *Lost and Founder*

Gary Keller, *The One Thing: The Surprisingly Simple Truth Behind Extraordinary Results*

Laurie Buchanan, *The Business of Being: Soul Purpose in and Out of the Workplace* and *Note To Self: A Seven Step Path to Gratitude and Growth*

Colleen Story, *Writer Get Noticed: A Strength Based Approach to Creating Author Platform* and *Overwhelmed Writer Rescue*

Stephen King, *On Writing*

Ann Lamont, *Bird by Bird*

Dave Farland: *Million Dollar Outlines* and *Million Dollar Book Signings*

Larry Brooks, *Story Engineering*

Jessica Brody, *Save The Cat! Writes a Novel*

JOIN THE CONVERSATION

WE TALKED a lot here about writing as a business, but there is so much more that can be said, and that we can learn from each other. Want to share your thoughts or learn what other writers think? Follow the hashtag #writingasabusiness on your favorite social media channel. Let's start a conversation!

Also be sure to visit and follow our blog at writingasabusiness.troy-lambertwrites.com. Have an idea to contribute? Reach out and your article could be featured. It's also a great way to build your brand and get another valuable backlink to your site.

ABOUT THE AUTHOR

Troy Lambert is a full-time writer and author. Having written over two dozen mysteries and other novels, Troy is well-versed in story creation, and he knows what it takes to make a fictional story real! Troy's hobbies and pastimes (when he's able to break away from the computer) include hiking into the mountains of South-west Idaho, fishing in a fast-rushing stream, and going for a drive where his mind can work on creating that perfect twist to the book he's currently writing.Troy and his wife live in Meridian, Idaho. You can find his other works, including his latest book, *Harvested*, at fictionupdates.troylambertwrites.com.

Made in the USA
Middletown, DE
26 September 2020

20605447R00163